Other publications by John Newell:

LET IT OUT

Train Your Voice to Be Free, Free Your Voice to Be Trained

A handbook for improving your singing.

2013

Available through Amazon in paperback, e-book, and audiobook.

DEPRESSION SURVIVOR

Blog

www.depression-survivor.com

John Newell

CLIMBING
THE MOUNTAIN

A survivor's guide to
overcoming depression.

ISBN 978-0-9920078-2-9 (paperback)
ISBN 978-0-9920078-3-6 (electronic edition)

Front cover design by Kirsten O'Dea of Kirsten Jane Design.

www.depression-survivor.com

www.facebook.com/climbingthemountain

To Corinne, Julie, Andrew, and Caitlyn.

You have my heart. I am forever grateful that you chose me and have never given up on me, even when I gave up on myself.

"Human life begins on the far side of despair."

— Jean-Paul Sartre, *The Flies*

"I was blaming instead of taking responsibility. I was taking the easy route that led nowhere instead of taking the hard one that led somewhere."

— Maxime Lagacé

"You can't stay in your corner of the forest waiting for others to come to you. You have to go to them sometimes."

— A.A. Milne, *Winnie the Pooh*

"Nobody else can destroy you except you; nobody else can save you except you."

— Osho, *The Empty Boat: Encounters with Nothingness*

"Unless someone like you cares a whole awful lot, nothing is going to get better. It's not."

— Dr. Seuss, *The Lorax*

"I believe depression is legitimate. But I also believe that if you don't exercise, eat nutritious food, get sunlight, get enough sleep, consume positive material, surround yourself with support, then you aren't giving yourself a fighting chance."

— attributed to Jim Carrey

Table of Contents

Introduction

Living with depression is hard. There's no sugar coating it. The heavy darkness of depression affects everything: your energy, your self-esteem, your will, your relationships, your work, your physical health, your personal life, your social life, your spiritual life, your sex life, your studies, your hobbies, and more.

Depression takes the joy out of life. It isolates you in a mental prison that seemingly nobody can penetrate. It skews your judgment and decision making. It strips away your enthusiasm for things you used to love. It distracts you from important tasks. It entices you to hide yourself away in misery. It encourages you to engage in destructive activities just to dull the pain for a moment, like drinking, taking drugs, smoking, vaping, gambling, reckless behaviour, and more. It pushes you to seek out conflict and outrage, subconsciously acting out against who wronged you or what traumatized you and clinging to the hurt. It convinces you that you deserve pain or that you should harm yourself. It makes you feel like you are trapped in an endless, unbreakable cycle of all these things, leaving you feeling alone, helpless, hopeless, and enveloped in shame and exhaustion.

Depression is quite simply a mountain. A massive, heavy, foreboding mountain. It sits on top of you, pushing you into the ground, weighing down on your mental and bodily functioning. The words "depressed" and "depression" are literally correct.

As somebody who developed depression in 1982 and has lived with it since, I know its effects only too well.

Unfortunately, depression won't go away by itself. We all wish it could.

How long and how badly you suffer from depression depends on what you *do* about it. That's right, to get the measure of depression, you have to do something. Many things, in fact. The actions you take – and don't take – determine your destiny with depression. Now, I know that taking action is probably the last thing you feel like doing. I get it. I'm so familiar with that feeling of all-consuming apathy; of being alone in an ocean of shame, thinking it's a safe cocoon. Said Henry Rollins, "I'll never forget how the depression and loneliness felt good and bad at the same time. Still does." (Rollins, 1998) I know only too well what it feels like to stay shut away and not try, and to lash out at or push away any- one who tries to get me up and do something different. Taking action fosters brain activity and thought patterns that can feel unfamiliar and scary. But depression thrives on inaction. The combination of inaction and isolation provides the perfect conditions for depressive, diabolical thoughts to keep circulating and grow stronger. In short, staying at the bottom under the mountain's enormous weight means letting depres- sion rule you. You can't even run away from it; the mountain stays with you, looming over you, wherever you go.

Climbing the mountain is the only way to tame it or conquer it. I call it a mountain because trying to tackle depression can feel like climbing Mount Everest. It's a gigantic challenge that looks impossible. Even just *thinking* about climbing it is intimidating. But climb it you must if you truly want to get your depression under control and put it in perspective.

Climbing your Everest requires preparation, hard work, and help. That's what this book is about: ***how to climb that mountain.***

To climb your mountain of depression, you have to change. I don't mean that you want change to come along and happen to you, or for you. You have to change *you*. You have to change what you do and how you think. That's the challenge and the solution.

Looking online isn't much help. Nobody ever said they got over depression thanks to the Internet. Sure, online you can find plenty of information about the effects of depression (which you probably know already) along with basic treatment ideas that provide some help but only scratch the surface. It's much harder to find good material about *how* to actually make your way up the mountain. While research and understanding are good, more important is the *action* you take. And that action needs to take you to the most vulnerable place – the summit of the mountain – where you can begin to release what caused your depression in the first place.

Don't look for shortcuts. There aren't any. There is no helicopter that can fly you to the top of Mount Everest and deposit you on the summit. You must do the work to get there. You have to climb, one step at a time.

The good news is that it *can* be done and that experts *can* help. I believed for years that I couldn't do it. My belief was wrong. I learned differently, thanks to so many helpful people and thanks to putting in a crap ton of effort.

You can do it – if you truly want to.

There is no prescribed timetable, so don't be concerned if it takes you a long time. More than three decades went by before I even made a proper start, let alone progress. Simply make the choice to climb the mountain and not give up. Sometimes you will stumble. Sometimes you will face huge challenges. Sometimes storms will force you back and you'll feel like you're covering the same ground, even starting again. I hope through this book you can develop more resilience and keep climbing. I say "more" because you are already amazingly resilient. You have carried and dragged your mountain around with you for a long time and you're still here trying to do something about it. That takes almost superhuman strength and perseverance. It proves that you have the strength to climb the mountain. Depression tries to convince you that you're weak, all the while that you're lugging its enormous weight around.

Listen to that small voice inside that says you can do it. The voice that says you can't is your past holding you prisoner. Your past is not your future, unless you allow it to be. What happened before was a lesson, not a life sentence. You *can* do this. I used to think I couldn't. And I was right – until I changed that thinking.

Do your best to get out of the cycle of saying how miserable you are. While talking about your feelings is important, you must also take action to change. That means you need to do both: discuss your feelings to lighten your load a little, then take accompanying action to get you moving up the mountain. In the end, your actions and behaviour will be what really count. As someone who excelled for nearly four decades at thinking how miserable I was, I can tell you that repeating over and over how awful things are only invites more misery. Trying to change depression is difficult, but it's not as damaging and debilitating as enduring misery upon misery for years.

Release all your expectations and focus on taking a step up your mountain right now. Whatever that step is, concentrate on taking it, nothing else. It's easy to become obsessed with an end result when what you need to do is focus on the process and the moment.

If you stumble or get distracted, shelve your guilt, no matter how hard it tries to drag you down. Would you put guilt on someone you care about who was in the same situation? Or would you give them love, encouragement, and a chance to start again? The moment of now is everlasting and provides you with a continuous, non-judgmental opportunity to pick yourself up, start fresh, and keep going. Use it.

At the end of your climb, a very different life awaits you. A life you hadn't considered or thought possible. Go get it!

Yes, Everest

I chose the Mount Everest analogy for good reasons.

- ☑ Just figuring out how to begin tackling your depression feels like stepping out from under a gigantic shadow to find that you're staring up at Mount Everest, the tallest, most intimidating mountain on the planet. It's so daunting that it looks too hard, too much, impossible. Depression thrives on impossible. It loves nothing more than to convince you that things *can't* be done and that nothing will ever get better. It will do everything in its power to keep you sedentary and stuck where you are.

- ☑ Why climb the mountain? Because it's there! Like Everest, your depression is the largest, most dominating feature of your life's landscape.
  - o You can climb it or you can be overshadowed and weighed down by it.
  - o You cannot make it go away, nor can you go around it. Either you make the choice to go over it or it will continue to stand in your way.

- ☑ You probably think you could never climb Mount Everest. It's dangerous, difficult, and arduous. Even when you're close to the summit, it can still seem so far. But many people have climbed Everest and many people have overcome depression. Why not you? It's not impossible. It *can* be done.

- ☑ Climbing Mount Everest requires training, a team, a guide, and a support system. So does tackling depression.

- ☑ There are thousands of steps to take, both up and down that mountain. Sometimes you will progress slowly and other times quickly. Sometimes you will make progress and other times you will encounter delays, setbacks, and failures. You succeed by taking one step at a time. Don't look at the huge mountain, focus on the next step, and keep going.

☑ Climbing Everest involves an unknown and unseeable goal. You're chasing a feeling/reality you've never known. You cannot imagine the greatness that might lie ahead.

☑ Successfully climbing will be your most transformational achievement. Those who have climbed Everest will never see the world the way they used to. They cannot go back to their old ways.

☑ You're not alone. Many others are climbing at the same time as you. Support each other, learn from each other. Accept the support and advice of others because it could be invaluable.

☑ Climbing the mountain doesn't make it disappear. Instead, you tame it. You see it differently. It no longer casts a spell over you.

☑ There are many other similarities to Everest that you'll see through this book.

My climb and your climb

I was sitting on the edge of my bed, isolating myself and trying to recover after a two-hour talk with my wife that included plenty of me screaming and crying. Another wave of heavy, dark shame had claimed me. I knew it well. The darkness was so familiar. The feeling of being crushed into the ground by an enormous weight was something I'd experienced for decades. That weight felt like a mountain, huge and immovable. It was made even worse because I knew my wife was also struggling at her wits' end, not knowing how to support me or even get through to me.

But a small voice somewhere in my mind told me life shouldn't be like this. It also said that the problem wouldn't go away by itself. If I wanted that mountain off my back, I had to do something different. I couldn't continue on the same old path and expect anything to improve. There had to be a way.

So, I went to see a psychologist. That was 2016. Amazingly, after 34 years of living with depression and all those dark episodes, I'd never been to a proper therapist. I wasn't convinced it would help, but I went. At long last I'd grasped that merely putting up with depression was not normal and I surely wasn't put on this planet to carry it forever. It was up to me to change things, nobody else. I didn't know how. I didn't know what I would face. I simply knew I had to try something different.

Now, five years later, I've learned to understand my depression, manage it, and change my life for the better.

Is depression gone from me forever? No. Does it rule me in the same way it used to? That's an even bigger *NO*. I will always have the memories of it all and I still have my triggers, but depression is no longer my master.

Back in 2016, I finally understood that what I needed was to change my approach. I had spent long enough actively resisting the will of the universe, flatly refusing even to listen to it. I had isolated myself in my depression prison and in the process lost my true self. 34 years it took me to grasp that I needed to make changes. I guess at some things I'm a slow learner. Or perhaps I was meant to carry the burden for such a long time so that I could become wiser for it and help others.

When it comes to depression, there's nothing special about me. I'm not a doctor, I'm not an expert, and it's not like I've had some unique version of depression like a rare strain of a disease. While I've dealt with great difficulties, many people have endured much more severe trauma. It's just that I've carried depression for a long, long time. I know what it's like from the inside and I've learned from every step of my climb up the mountain.

I was 12 when I developed depression. Over the next 20 to 30 years, I never really understood it or how to approach it. Sure, sometimes I sought out advice and help. I spoke to doctors, took medication, read some books, exercised on and off, experimented with a full spectrum happy lamp, and tried to make some changes. I did everything short of actually changing myself. Don't get me wrong, those things I did were (and are) excellent support tools. They're just not the answer and I shouldn't have expected them to be. Add to that, in the 1990s and early 2000s approaches to depression weren't as developed, at least not in the circles I moved in. It wasn't a subject people talked about openly for fear of ridicule and reprisal. It was still seen by many as weakness or even "craziness", not at all a legitimate affliction or illness. Treatment was all about just that: treatment. There wasn't much in the mainstream about how to delve into the *cause* of depression and release its grasp. I naïvely thought I could beat my depression by myself. It was naïve only because I didn't know what I was doing, didn't grasp what I was up against, and didn't think I needed psychiatric help. As a result, I suffered over many years. People around me suffered as well. I kept myself at a distance from my family. I cut people out of my life, sometimes blaming them and clinging to my hurt, and other times blaming myself for being an unworthy loser. I became a mixture of cynical, bitter, and withdrawn. I didn't advance professionally the way I wanted. I lost many friends. I lost a marriage. I lost myself. I went on and off medication, but that was about the extent of professional treatment I pursued.

Then along came 2016. I experienced a trigger that sent me into the blackest pit I'd ever been in. I'd experienced depressive episodes many times before, but this one felt even stronger. A desperate darkness engulfed me to my core. I questioned everything I'd ever done in my life and questioned my worth as a husband, as a father, and as a man. I blamed myself for everything that I didn't think was the way it should be in my life, yet I projected my shame and rage onto others around me and vomited my emotions on them in very ugly fashion. I saw myself as unworthy, unloved, and unlovable. I couldn't even accept the love of my wife when she offered it. I felt cast back to being a child and a teenager again. I relived the parts of my upbringing when I thought I was the lowest rung on the ladder in my family and believed I had no identity other than one that met the expectations of key people in my life.

It wasn't the fault of those other people. It wasn't anybody's fault. Yes, people had very high expectations of me, but as a boy I wasn't mentally equipped with the tools to deal with it all. So, I unknowingly allowed the expectations to pile on top of me and shape how I thought, how I behaved, and what I thought of myself.

In 2016, when those feelings of darkness, desolation, and hopelessness struck me so powerfully, I was intensely frustrated that this was still happening to me after 34 years. I'd reached breaking point. But it was also at this moment that a different thought struck me... *My life shouldn't be like this!* There had to be a reason why I was still dealing with depression. The fact that it kept recurring over and over told me I must have been approaching it wrong all those years. It became clear I could no longer do the things I'd done before, like merely treating the symptoms, or even accepting depression as a permanent condition that

I could only "manage" rather than defeat. (After all, I wasn't managing it.) If I wanted this shit to stop, I had to *do something different*. I had to break the cycle. The universe was sending me a message that things must change. In fact, it had been sending me that message for 34 years – my depression was the messenger – but I hadn't listened.

So, I called a psychologist and booked an appointment. I began a journey of uncovering *why* I had depression and what had incited it. No longer would I treat only the symptoms; I would find the cause and treat that.

I began climbing my mountain.

The climb was fraught with fear and frustration, despair and desperation, exasperation and exhaustion. As I took steps up my mountain, I felt like I was getting closer to the cause of my depression and yet also getting nowhere. There were many times in my climb that I stood still and thought I couldn't take another step. Frequently I looked up the mountain and thought, "This is too much... It's too far... It's too hard... I'll never get there..." I slipped and stumbled over and over, each time thinking I was falling all the way to the bottom, back to square one. I became engulfed by storms that made me rage at everyone and the world, to the point of pounding wildly on the floor and yelling hysterically. And there were many occasions when I decided to stop and stay where I was, thinking that I was better off to just stop trying.

But each time, usually a day or two later, I regathered my thoughts, stood up, and took another step. A shaky step, but a step nonetheless. Sometimes that step involved talking to someone and unburdening some of my troubles for a moment. A lightened or shared load could help me climb better. Most frequently, that next step involved doing the repetitive work my psychologist asked me to do. I did that work, over and over, not knowing where I was going with it, just trusting that it would eventually help. After all, my psychologist was an expert who knew the mountain very well.

Then, as I approached what I thought was the summit, yet more fierce storms hit. They pummeled me, belted me, beat me down. Each time I felt deflated and defeated. But somehow I rode out those storms, got up again, and took one more step. A few times I knew I was close to the summit – close to knowing the exact cause of my depression and how to release it. But there were still more obstacles, illusions, and storms. The peak was indeed close, yet farther away than I thought. All I could do was continue taking one step at a time. That approach had brought me this far and I wasn't going to waste all the effort I'd put in.

At last, when I did reach the summit, it wasn't what I expected. There was no "Aha!" moment (unlike Freud had said), no great revelation, no single thing I could point to. The cause of my depression had been more than one thing. I learned that how my depression developed was more complicated and subtle than I'd imagined. Still, from the top of my personal Mount Everest, I saw things differently. It became clear that I had believed bad things about myself for too long. I'd been trained over the years – first by others, then by myself – to believe I was unworthy, to submit to shame, and to believe (often subconsciously) that bad things would continue happening to me. On the summit, I began the work to release the negative and destructive beliefs I'd held about myself for many years. I began releasing the old ways that had left me at the mercy of depression. I began learning to forgive myself and to forgive others. And I felt closer to the place where I could live the life I'm supposed to live.

Of course, my trek wasn't over just because I'd stood on the peak of my mountain. I wasn't "cured". Successfully climbing a mountain means successfully coming back down. I still had much more work to do. But at last I knew why I had suffered for decades and that I could do something about it.

In one way for me, it will never be over. My mountain is still there. It won't disappear just because I climbed it. But now I look at it differently. It stands as a visible reminder of so much. I see it as a messenger that told me for years to change my ways. It could even turn out to be a blessing.

Through my climb, I learned that depression had isolated me – or more accurately, that I had isolated myself. For years, people had described me as distant, aloof, guarded, arrogant. Aloof was a big one. I stayed away from people whenever I could, in a bid to avoid being hurt again. When I had no choice but to be in social situations, I put on a front because I'd been trained since childhood that that was expected of me. I judged people, wrongly thinking that finding fault in them and cutting them down might make me feel validated and valuable.

In many ways I'm still isolated from others. I'm working on that. Only through connection can we humans find joy and be fruitful. When we lose connectivity with others, suffering always occurs.

You will find *your* journey to be much like I've described above and throughout this book. The details of your story will be different from mine, but the clarity and perspective you gain should be similar. When you reach the summit of your Mount Everest, you will understand that your beliefs about yourself are at the root of your depression. You will know how and why those beliefs were conditioned into you. You will grasp that depression isn't an intrinsic part of you – it's an entity of its own that you can learn to separate from your true self.

I say "when" and "will" about your climb up the mountain because I know you can climb it. You can. The fact that you're reading this means you haven't given up and you want to do something about your depression.

Be sure you look for solutions, not just treatments – and learn the difference. It's easy to find basic treatment advice for depression. There are lots of tips out there. But those treatment ideas represent only some of the *equipment* and *tools* you must carry when you climb the mountain. They aren't the map to the summit. Don't get me wrong, some of those treatment ideas are excellent and you should definitely use the ones that help you. Just understand that they help you feel better prepared and equipped for the climb. Treatments don't undertake the climb for you.

When you go searching for a pathway to the summit of your mountain, you'll find there isn't much online or in books about how to really get stuck into that journey and how to weather the storms that will hit. Nor will you find much advice about how to overcome the resistance you feel to climbing the mountain in the first place. Why is there so little detailed help in those places?

1. **Because your journey is your own.** It's *your* mountain. It might be similar to other depressed people's mountains, but it's unique nonetheless. Your route to the summit will follow a unique path. While you might prepare, train, and carry the same equipment as anybody else who has depression, there are personal challenges that you must overcome in order to succeed.

2. **Because you need professional help and a support team.** There's simply no climbing Mount Everest without help and support. You must choose your team. People who know you. People who know your triggers, your motivations, your issues, your joys, your fears, your strengths, your weaknesses. They are the people who can guide you and walk with you and cheer for you on your unique pathway.

It's time to climb. Your mountain has weighed on you long enough. Let's get started!

ONE

Decide to act

STOP! Go no farther unless you truly want to change and are prepared to act on it.

If you aren't prepared to make changes, you're wasting your time.

This is your mountain. Nobody can climb it for you and it won't go away by itself.

You must choose: stay where you are or start climbing. You know what the former feels like, only too well.

To climb your mountain, you must decide three things:
- That you want to reframe your depression.
- That you want to change.
- That you must act.

1. Decide to reframe your depression

Your depression didn't arise because bad things happened to you or because you're a "bad" person. It developed out of what you believe about yourself *in response* to traumatic things that happened. The thought patterns that became habitual after trauma are the key. Depressive episodes keep recurring because of those thought patterns and their associated emotional memories. That means changing those thought patterns is essential to making positive progress.

During an episode of depression, negative mood occurs alongside negative thinking and bodily sensations of sluggishness and fatigue. When the episode is past, and the mood has returned to normal, the negative thinking and body sensations tend to disappear as well. However, during the episode an association has been learned between the various symptoms. This means that when negative mood happens again (for any reason) it will tend to trigger all the other symptoms in proportion to the strength of association (this is called 'differential activation'). When this happens, the old habits of negative thinking will start up again, negative thinking gets into the same rut, and a full-blown episode of depression may be the result.

The discovery that, even when people feel well, the link between negative moods and negative thoughts remains ready to be re-activated, is of enormous importance. It means that sustaining recovery from depression depends on learning how to keep mild states of depression from spiralling out of control.

(Centre for Suicide Research, University of Oxford, 2013)

To reframe your depression, acknowledge that there is a problem and, more importantly, that you can do something about it. If you think your depression is inevitable, predestined, unavoidable, permanent, or even genetic, then you have some powerful excuses. Telling yourself such things creates beliefs that will continue to come true and shape your reality.

Decide that you can challenge your beliefs about depression.

Depression is about what happened in the past. Anxiety is about the future. The past doesn't exist anymore and the future is not set. But you can change and reframe your *present moment* to shape how you deal with your past and approach your future.

2. Decide to change

Be careful here. I don't mean that you want change, like you want change to happen. Or like you want your pain taken away – everybody with depression wants that. That's like asking to be deposited on the mountain's peak without doing anything to get yourself there. It's not a desire for change, it's a desire *to* change. You must want to change *you*. Then you must do something to tackle the source of your pain.

Q. How many psychologists does it take to change a light bulb?

A. Only one, but the light bulb must *want* to change.

This old joke is true. It's easy to scoff at it as just a throwaway cliché if you mistakenly think a therapist will simply give you the solution to your depression. Many people get disheartened in counselling because they expect the therapist to hand them an answer or cure. Sorry, nobody can do that. What a therapist *can* do is show you a pathway and provide help and support for you to walk it. The professional helps open a doorway; you're the one who must go through it.

At times, as you strive to change, the climb up the mountain will be steep. You will come face to face with some difficult personal stuff. You will be tested and challenged to the max. There will be moments when you will think the climb is too hard and will want to give up. That's because you will be confronting deeply held beliefs and deeply rooted shame. You will be trying to "rewire" your thoughts and your depression will fight you with everything it's got.

Your desire to change must not waver. You simply have to want to make yourself different, to change your way of thinking, to reprogram your mind. You must want to release everything that has kept you at depression's mercy.

3. Take action

Thoughts and good intentions are not enough. Actions count. Only through action can you climb your mountain. Without action, your Mount Everest will continue to loom over you. To climb it, you must take a lot of small steps, one after another. Forget the distant summit of the mountain for a moment. Just take the next step. It's about making progress.

There are two simple actions to take immediately:

- Arrange an appointment with a clinical professional in the field of mental health. (More about this in the Sherpa chapter.)
- Enroll family or friends to be your active supporters and cheerleaders as you work on making changes. Invite them to help you explore new possibilities in your life and participate in a

new story about who you are. If you are somebody who regularly turns to loved ones to complain or to dump emotions on them, this is a very different approach filled with positive possibilities.

Don't make elaborate plans right now to reschedule your life. There's no need to overthink, which can talk you out of taking action. Just do these two things.

Many people fall in love with the *idea* of climbing the mountain without actually doing it. They toy with a few treatment tools without committing and without taking any actual steps, believing that that's how it's done or believing they're doing enough. It's like how people fall in love with the idea of losing weight but don't make enough real changes – or have too many cheat days or follow a program that doesn't work for them – and wonder why they struggle to make progress.

Taking action is a leap of faith. You won't know exactly where you are going. That's okay. Although it is scary and uncertain, keep taking action, again and again. That's how to make wholesale changes in your mental programming. You must break the cycle of thinking that has kept you enslaved to depression.

Of course, when you do take action, your depression is going to push back and tell you it's too hard and too much work. It will do everything it can to convince you that climbing the mountain is a hopeless cause. That you can't do it. That there's no point even trying. That it's too painful. That it's easier to stay where you are and cover up and feel "safe". That you should have another drink or hit of drugs. That you should feel ashamed and guilty. That depression is your destiny for the rest of your life.

Bullshit!

Staying still and numbing yourself, or worse doing self-destructive things, achieves nothing good. Instead it makes you feel lower, holds you in a cycle of shame, and keeps you away from the life you could be living.

It's okay for you to tell your depression that it's talking bullshit.

Defiance can be a huge factor in motivating you to act. So can simply being fed up with depression, like I was. Other motivators might be family, friends, love, work, the example of others, a desire to help somebody, even something as small as reading an inspirational quote.

You know that your depression will resist your actions. Depression wants you to stay imprisoned. You have lived in that prison for a long time; you know how it feels. Staying inside it is pointless and destructive. The only way to break out and get something different is to *do* something different.

Put your heart and soul into action, even when things go against you and the way forward is scary and unclear. Just like climbing Mount Everest, overcoming depression requires total focus and commitment, one small step at a time.

And keep taking action daily, even after you return from your climb. Depression can sneak back if you stop. What you learn from climbing the mountain, you need to keep doing forever after.

Act now

Don't wait until you're "ready". Depression won't let you feel ready. Motivation won't come as if by magic. Do one thing now that could help your depression: make an appointment, call a supporter, eat better, drink some water, go for a walk, meditate, anything. Fight through the depression telling you to stay put and give up.

> Beating ourselves up about all the things we think we're doing wrong becomes a litany that turns into white noise, until we don't even hear it anymore.
>
> — Rachel Hollis

(Hollis R. , 2018)

TWO

The phases of your journey

Accepting	You acknowledge that you have depression; that the mountain is looming over you and is affecting your entire life. Accepting that the mountain is even there can be a great personal challenge. Some people are held back by stigma and shame about mental illness. Others refuse to acknowledge that it exists or that it could affect them.
Deciding to Act	Choosing to do something rather than let depression rule you forever. Making the commitment to yourself to have a go.
Seeking Guidance	Seeing mental health professionals. Reading and researching about depression. Looking to mentors and role models. Joining support groups, taking classes, and attending appointments and meetings.
Preparing	Readying your support team and supplies. Acknowledging the life changes you must make when you attempt the climb to conquer depression.
Climbing	The most arduous phase that can take the longest time. This is where you do the repetitive work your mental health professionals ask you to do.
The Summit	Understanding the cause of your depression. Making the commitment to release and forgive.
Climbing Down	The work you put in for the rest of your changed life to forgive yourself and others, and ensure you keep depression in its proper place and perspective. The depression will never be erased, just like a mountain cannot be levelled, but you can teach yourself to see it differently.

THREE

Change your mindset

To climb this mountain, you must:

- **Really want to do it. If this makes you respond negatively – "I've wanted to do this for years! Screw you, John!" – work on** *believing* **you can climb. Desire without belief is just a wish.**
- **Grasp how depression tries to convince you that you can't climb the mountain and that trying is pointless.**
- **Open your mind to new ideas, approaches, advice, activities, and people.**
- **Take action over and over again.**

To change your mindset:

- **Strive to eliminate false, unprofitable beliefs about depression.**
- **Stop identifying with depression.**
- **Avoid using your depression as a crutch or excuse.**
- **Focus on behaviour instead of labels.**
- **Understand that depression is a messenger.**
- **Don't assume you know why you have depression.**
- **Accept your feelings.**
- **Do something. Take action.**
- **Shift your paradigm to change your self-beliefs.**
- **Accept help.**
- **Celebrate good moments and be grateful for them.**

No problem can be solved from the same level of consciousness that created it.

— Albert Einstein

Y ou cannot climb a mountain if you believe it's impossible. Changing your mindset is like upgrading your brain's software. It's one of the biggest challenges with depression and requires repetition and reprogramming over an extended time. However long it took to develop the mindset that has fed your depression, it may take just as long to completely reprogram it. You must prepare, train, learn, adapt, and persist just like a mountain climber. You also need to learn the tricks depression will play on you and how to make good decisions to overcome those tricks.

> What you desire has been deliberately placed out of reach so that you can become the person it takes to obtain it. Don't buy into the limitations of your current circumstances.
>
> — Author unknown

Refer back to this chapter when you are climbing. It lists some typical mindset blockages and contains many actions for you to take to clear those blockages, both during your ascent up the mountain and during your climb back down. As you battle your old ways of thinking and face many triggers and obstacles, use this chapter as a reminder that your repeated thoughts and beliefs control your mental health.

Ultimately, changing your mindset means *taking action*, just like climbing a mountain does. If you do nothing, nothing will change. To tackle depression, you must behave differently. And behaving differently is how you go about learning to think differently.

It's not easy. I hate to say that because no doubt you feel unmotivated, beaten down, and exhausted from your depression. You might feel overwhelmed by the enormity of the task and how much effort it will take. I totally get it. I've been there so many times.

Think only of one step at a time. Put the destination out of your mind. Put past failures out of your mind. This is huge for depression and requires a lot of practice. Tackling depression – and anxiety, for that matter – requires learning to live in the present moment. Depression keeps you reliving your past in fear and shame, convincing you that whatever has happened before will happen again. You cannot change the past and trying to change it is an exercise in futility. Meanwhile, anxiety makes you worry about things that haven't happened yet, which is also a waste of energy. *Now* is what we have. The moment of now lasts forever. Now is where and when we live. And the moment of now provides an endless and non-judgmental opportunity to renew. So take that one step now. That is all that is required at this moment. Be assured that it can be done.

Don't try to force the process of changing how you think. In a way, it's like being born. It feels enormously scary and painful as you are about to enter a reality you have never known. The change will come when you allow yourself to be vulnerable and listen to the will of the universe.

Strive to eliminate false, unprofitable beliefs

Over the years, I've thought and believed all of the things listed below. I'm sure you've thought many of them as well.

- *"There's no point. It will never work. I tried before and failed. Nothing will change."* Your history is not your future unless you allow it to be. You didn't fail. You made some progress up the mountain and got turned back. You can still climb it.
- *"Mental illness is all through my family background, therefore it's inevitable that I have it."* This false belief is an excuse. Your depression is never inevitable. You have the power to choose your reality.
- *"It's genetic."* This relates to the false belief above about depression being inevitable. There is some evidence to support the idea that certain people carry a gene that may make them more susceptible to developing depression, but that's hardly a guar-

antee. Conditioning and belief play the largest roles in depression.

- *"I am to blame for having depression."* Not true. I wasn't. Neither are you. You are never to blame. Blame answers nothing and solves nothing.
- *"Depression is who I am."* Depression is not a permanent part of you or a life sentence, unless you allow it to be.
- *"Depression rules my life."* You have the power to put depression in its place and grow from it.
- *"I'll never beat depression. I give up."* If you believe that, you will be right. Every time. Belief creates reality.
- *"I'll feel better when XYZ happens."* While some circumstances may be triggering your depressive episodes or causing you great stress right now, your mental health is not dependent upon those circumstances improving. You won't have depression lifted magically away if external conditions improve. You'll still need to work on your self-beliefs, your internal narratives, and your emotional wounds. Said Naval Ravikant, the entrepreneur and Fellow of the Edmund Hillary Fellowship, "The fundamental delusion – there is something out there that will make me happy and fulfilled forever."
- *"The best I can hope for is to manage it a bit."* Have you ever wondered why some people can get on top of their depression and why you seem to be stuck? It's time to open your mind. Your mind enabled depression to take root and your mind has the power to remove those roots.
- *"Having depression is shameful."* Why? Depression is common. It's very often rooted in shame, a learned (not innate) emotion that is very destructive. Bill Clinton said, "Mental illness is nothing to be ashamed of, but stigma and bias shame us all."
- *"Depression is weakness."* On the contrary, it takes incredible strength to carry the burden of depression. That strength can be used to shed it.

- *"Medication will fix it."* Medication is a helpful tool, not a cure. If you've been prescribed medication, use it in conjunction with many other tools.
- *"Changing is too hard."* What is truly hard is living with the stress and the anxiety of depression all the time 24/7. It drains your energy and life force. Ultimately, you are the most important thing in your life. Working on your mental health is the most important thing you can do.
- *"Isolating and protecting myself is essential. Shutting out people, emotions, and even hope will keep me safe."* Isolation worsens depression. Reach out, ask for help, and accept help. You must be vulnerable, which feels terrifying and makes you think you'll get hurt worse than ever. But erecting big walls around yourself keeps depression inside. You must dismantle those walls, even if you don't know what your new life will look like.
- *"This is just an attempt to get me hooked into the pharmaceutical system."* If you think every doctor's primary motivation is to make money from drugs, you are more likely to believe other unprofitable ideas that will hold you back. Open your mind to every possibility that might help in some small way.

Stop identifying with depression

You experience depression. You are not depression.

See the difference?

Depression is not who you are. It is not your defining characteristic. You are not your wounds and you are not your trauma. Wounds and trauma happened to you, but how you view them is key to moving forward and climbing your mountain.

Depression has nothing to do with your identity or your character, unless you allow it. It's very easy to develop the mentality whereby your depression is a special feature that sets you apart. After all, with it you can get attention (even the negative kind), which can make you feel validated on some level. Even the satisfaction of telling a helpful person to leave you alone means you have received attention and brings a twisted sense of validation, even power.

When you see a meme or quote about how awful a person with depression feels, it's easy to think, "Yep, that's me." Although the meme or quote may be true and you might feel relieved because somebody "gets it" about how you're feeling, when you think, "That's me," you put yourself in a box. It's like you and depression become one. This way of thinking can allow depression to seep into your sense of identity. In today's online world, it's easy to seek out memes and quotes about how bad you feel and how depression has you in its grip. It's just as easy to post them on social media, especially as they can garner attention, thus making you feel validated. Once in a while is okay; we all need to reach out for support and help. But continued repetition can let the belief seep in that depression "belongs" to you and that it's an integral and permanent part of who you are. Most times, putting negative thoughts out there online has no positive effect. What truly helps is taking proper action. Every time you see a post saying how depression makes a person feel isolated, insignificant, and shameful, agreeing with it can subconsciously tell yourself to stay depressed. Seeing such posts over and over, day after day, creates a self-pity party of circular thinking. Breaking that circle is essential for tackling your depression mountain.

If you must put it out there to people that you're feeling terrible, actively *ask* for support and then *accept* it. Talking about your problems is a good thing to do, up to a point. Just be wary not to let the problems dominate your talking. Discuss ways forward and take action. Strive to change your perspective, change your beliefs, and change your thought patterns that focus on problems and on victimhood. Change the old station that's been playing in your head.

Therefore, don't look for quotes and memes that encourage you to wallow in depression and that provide an excuse not to try. Look for inspirational material that encourages you to *do something* to tackle your depression. Taking action is far better than defining yourself through recognition.

Depression is not your destiny. I remember many depressive episodes where I thought, "This is my lot. Nothing will get better. I'm stuck with depression for life." In those moments, I had decided that depression was part of who I was. Guess what happened? It persisted.

Depression is not your core problem. It's a symptom. You are not your wounds and it's time to break their hold on you.

Avoid using depression as an excuse or crutch

It's very easy to think of depression as a crutch to lean on or a hook to hang all your problems on. You end up wearing it as a convenient label and using it as an excuse to talk yourself out of things. "I can't do this task because I have depression... I can't go to that function because I'm depressed..." A diagnosis of depression does not explain away all problems. But by exploiting the excuse, you affirm depression as your master. In fact, you're exploiting the benefits of your depression. Now I can almost hear you yell, "What?! There are *no* benefits to depression! Fuck you, John!" Of course there are benefits. In the past, I used my depression to get attention and empathy, to get out of work and events, to avoid gatherings, to draw people into my drama, to cut others down to my level, to project my issues, and so on.

Of course, sometimes you won't be able to face a task or attend an event because you feel like crap and can barely get out of bed. That's okay, sometimes. I totally get it. But if you repeatedly tell yourself that you can't do things or can't join in because you have depression, then it's an excuse. You *can* do/attend those things. You're choosing not to.

> Depression does not rob you of the choice; it just tricks you into making the wrong one.
>
> — Mel Robbins

(Robbins, 2018)

If you spend days or weeks or months refusing to get up and try, that's a form of self-sabotage. Then depression becomes a crutch, an excuse not to help yourself. At that point, you're one step away from letting it take possession of your sense of self. Once that happens, it's so easy to give up entirely.

But ask yourself: Who is more important to help than you?

Focus on behaviour, not labels

With depression, it's disturbingly easy to use labels that define you and persecute you. "I'm depressed... I'm a born introvert... I'm not as good as that person... I'm a loser... I deserve it... Life will always suck." Please choose your words more mindfully when discussing your depression. Try not to say, "I am depressed." That makes it seem like a permanent condition and the label goes to your very core as a person. Instead, try saying, "I am a human being experiencing the emotions of depression right now." That focuses on what you are feeling without trying to define you. What you are experiencing are emotions that are short-lived, ephemeral, fleeting. Rather than hang a label on yourself, figure out different language that describes precisely what you're going through. In other words, don't catastrophize.

All labels and beliefs about your depression are rooted in shame. It's time to cast those labels and beliefs from your mind. Focus on how you *feel*, how you *behave*, what you *do*, how to *take action*, and stop judging yourself about it all. Negative judgment feeds the labels and shame that hold you in place.

Some days you will be able to take some action towards climbing your mountain. Other days you may not be able to. That's okay. Do "successful" days make you a good person? Do "unsuccessful" days make you a loser? To answer these questions, ask yourself if you would label somebody you care about in these ways. Of course you wouldn't! So stop judging and labeling yourself. You can even reframe what you regard as successful. Set the bar lower. Success doesn't have to mean getting an A, landing a new job, earning tons of money, or even taking a good selfie. When you're dealing with depression, success can be as simple as getting off the couch or getting dressed.

> Success is liking yourself, liking what you do, and liking how
> you do it.
>
> — Maya Angelou

Depression is a messenger

The messenger is telling you that something has to change. When you don't listen and resist change, the messenger comes back again and again, louder and louder.

When your depression started, you had been hurt. The trauma of that hurt caused you to put up mental barriers and develop strategies to defend yourself from being hurt again. That's perfectly natural and understandable. Trauma is overwhelming and difficult to process and comprehend. For a short while, those barriers served a purpose. They enabled you to survive the trauma, perhaps even carry on with life with some normality. However, the longer you kept those defensive barriers up, the more they kept unresolved feelings inside. Walls keep things out, but they also keep things in. Holding negative emotions inside, without processing and releasing them in a healthy way, contributed to the upheaval in the chemical balance in your brain and affected your perceptions and beliefs. Depression came along as a messenger to tell you that the defence strategies you created are no longer serving you. Celebrate those defensive measures for what they did to help you survive the initial trauma, but now it's time to let them go. It's time to change. If you don't change, the messenger will keep returning, louder and louder. You've already experienced that.

When you can see depression as a messenger, instead of a label or affliction, you realize it's not a life sentence. Do everything you can to sift through the mental "noise" so you can listen to the message and change your approach. The message is not something negative like "I suck" or "Everything sucks"; those views develop if the messenger is ignored. The true message is about something you must release and some action you must take.

The longer you ignore, shut out, or deny the message, the longer depression will stay.

Don't assume you know why you have depression

It's very common for people with depression to believe that their condition developed because negative things happened to them sometime in their past. But many people have endured great trauma without developing depression, so there must be a reason why they avoided it while others have been struck down.

I remember listening to the audiobook *Kick Ass* by Mel Robbins. One of the people Mel talked to was a sexual assault survivor who thought all her problems came down to that assault. Why? Because her therapist told her as much: "You were sexually abused and that's why you're depressed." That might seem logical at first, but it turned out she had different issues. Unfortunately, the therapist's statement allowed her to define herself by the traumatic incident, and thus her treatment didn't get to the root cause of her problems. The assault was horrendous and traumatic, but it became obvious in the audiobook recording that talking about certain other topics upset her far more than talking about the assault. Mel Robbins picked up on that and explored. It was amazing. It was a clear example of how any of us can blame the wrong issue or simply accept a diagnosis or label as the centre of our problems, instead of digging deeper. The most important thing Mel did for this woman was to empower her to change her behaviour. At that point, she was no longer a victim of her abuse. Instead she was in a new position of power over her own mind, because she understood that her reality had been created by her and not by her abuse.

For all of us dealing with depression, there has been an inciting incident (or perhaps several) that caused a core wound. Sometimes we can identify the inciting incident, and other times we blame another incident, like in the example above. Either way, we may focus intently on both the incident and the wound, and we may hang our troubles with depression on them. "I was abused... My parents got divorced...

My spouse cheated on me… I failed to get into university… I lost my job…" We all have a core wound where we think our parents or another significant person failed us or betrayed us or abandoned us at a key moment, leaving us feeling hurt, isolated, and marginalized. From such an incident, we cling to the hurt, replaying it over and over until we create a narrative that rebounds on ourselves in destructive fashion. Right there is the cause of depression: not the incident, but the *narrative* created in the mind.

In order to climb your mountain, at some point you must identify those hurtful inciting moments and go back and forgive. No good can come from clinging to this past hurt and keeping your thoughts rooted in this cycle. Otherwise, you're choosing to believe that you have depression because bad things happened to you. Depression developed due to how your mind *responded* and *adapted* to those bad things.

One way that you might have responded and adapted to traumatic events is to disconnect from others, in a bid to avoid being hurt again. This relates to the inciting incident mentioned above where, at a crucial moment, you felt like a key figure had failed, betrayed, or abandoned you. If it happened in your childhood or infancy, the detachment and disconnection may be repeated over and over in later life. How you attach with other people has a profound effect on your happiness and sense of self-worth. (By the way, how you attach with others bears strong resemblance to how you attach with parental figures.) If connection and attachment are broken in a traumatic way and you become isolated and withdrawn, physically and/or mentally, it's easy to develop negative self-image and to experience depression. We humans need to connect with each other. Whenever we lose connection or refuse to connect, suffering occurs. On the other hand, if we can learn how to process trauma and its associated effects and emotions, we can come through with better self-image and with continued positive connection to others. The good news is it's never too late to learn.

Some people, including me, have dealt with negative self-belief since early childhood. The core wound and the mental response to that wound go back to when they couldn't yet think in words but could form powerful emotional memories. A baby forms a profound bond with its parents, especially its mother who provides food, comfort, and love. Following the work of John Bowlby in the 1950s, research into attachment has shown that if a baby is left to "cry it out" for hours, it is an incredibly traumatic experience. The baby cannot understand why the parent is suddenly not responding or helping. Instead of putting 2 and 2 together like an adult would and figuring out that he/she can go to sleep and all will be well in the morning, the baby can only experience emotions of fear, catastrophe, abandonment, and betrayal because the key figure of life support has disappeared. This distress forms an indelible emotional memory that affects how the baby re-attaches to the parent and, later in life, affects attachment to others. As the baby grows, he/she can become less trusting of others, less content, less affectionate, more anxious, and more withdrawn, all of which diminish self-worth. "Something must be wrong with me!" is the typical kind of internal narrative that is formed in a child's mind, even at a purely emotional and non-verbal level. (Many people who have experienced this grow to develop impostor syndrome, whereby they cannot accept praise and success because they have responded to their core wound by constructing the "I suck" belief.) For people who have gone through such attachment/separation trauma as infants, it's common for them later to be afraid of trusting and attaching again, and therefore they isolate themselves or hold back from people, or even become aggressive in a bid to ward off being harmed again and avoid triggering negative memories. It's also common for them to attach too strongly to others as substitutes, becoming dependent and clingy to the point that those others feel smothered or overwhelmed and subsequently reject them.

Much of what I wrote in the previous paragraph has been true for me personally. For years, I thought (incorrectly) that my depression was caused by one event at age 12, mostly because it was the first time I had felt depression so intensely. When I turned 12 in 1982, my family moved 2,500 kilometres away from our home to a different state in

Australia. I did not want to move. It was upsetting and I hated it. But it wasn't the cause of my depression. It was a trigger. By the time I finally understood this, I was almost 50. Therapy, research, and reflection revealed to me that the roots of my depression were sown when I was a small boy. It was back then that I developed negative self-image. First, as a baby, I was left at night to cry it out a few times. Then I had been unknowingly conditioned over years to be shaped by shame, to have poor self-esteem, to create a façade, and to seek validation through the approval of authority figures. The big move in 1982 triggered my emotional memories of catastrophe from feeling utterly isolated. My life had been turned upside down, I knew nobody, and I couldn't turn to my parents for help. (That wasn't their fault, by the way. My father had a hugely responsible new job and my mother was trying to sort out our new lives and new house while caring for my life-threateningly ill brother.) Crucially, I had no idea how to process my feelings and no help to learn how. Instead, I put up mental barriers and intensified my negative internal narrative. Shame and anger were triggered within me and took over. Certain thoughts began to repeat again and again: "This sucks... I'm alone... I don't know anyone... It's hopeless... My parents did this to me and now they're not available... I'm helpless... Everyone hates me.... Nobody understands me..." I clung to the negative aspects, not moving beyond what happened and how much it hurt. Inevitably, my thoughts turned to "I must deserve this... There's something wrong with me... I suck..." I withdrew from everyone. Little did I know that these patterns had taken root in my infancy and childhood. And, of course, those thoughts, emotions, and actions became self-fulfilling. What I put out, I got back. And I blamed the wrong issue. Bear in mind, at 12 I was still a child without more sophisticated thought processes and without any tools to help me change my thinking.

Now, after intensive reflection, I can look back and see that factors not related to my family's big move were at the core of my depression. (Importantly, I have moved beyond the blame mentality that kept me anchored to depression.) As a boy, I lived with restrictions that other kids didn't and I had to live up to very high expectations. If I didn't live up to those expectations, I felt ashamed. I copied my older brothers singing in the church choir because I had noticed the praise and recognition they received from my mother for how their accomplishments and behaviour reflected well on our family. When I joined the choir and lived up to expectations, I received the same praise. But when I didn't behave as expected and when I was disciplined (in everyday life, not merely in choir and church), I felt great shame. I was a good singer in the choir, but I look back and see that for much of the time I put on a front in order to gain praise or to avoid shame. It was inauthentic. I unknowingly equated praise with love and equated meeting another person's expectations with my self-worth. (Through much of my life, I continued seeking the recognition and praise of others in order to feel valid.) Meanwhile, when I was disciplined as a child, I was usually isolated ("Go to your room!"), where dark thoughts of anger and shame could fester. The intent was to have me cool off, which I kind of did, but it also turned out to be an ideal way to revive my emotional memories of "cry it out" abandonment. Because I was a child, I didn't think, "What's wrong with this situation? What can I do differently?" My child mind could only be petulantly angry at my parents and at the world before turning the negativity on myself and thinking, "What's wrong with *me*?" When I emerged from my room, I was expected to say sorry while rules and expectations were reinforced. I didn't have an outlet for my negative emotions, nor did I learn how to move forward in a healing way. I don't blame my parents. They're wonderful people with no ill intent. They're also imperfect human beings who did the best they could with what they knew under stressful circumstances, just like any parents. They love me and I love them. Ultimately, I had *taught myself* for years to believe that I was an "unwanted" little boy. I had *taught myself* to look outside myself for happiness, equating recognition with love; while when I made mistakes, I learned to feel ashamed, isolated and unworthy. It's no wonder I had difficulty adapting to our move, developing lasting friendships, maintaining relationships, and so on.

That's why I developed depression. Not because my family moved, but because poor self-esteem and destructive habits had been ingrained into me as a child, albeit inadvertently. I then spent years cementing those habits into beliefs. I sabotaged myself and isolated myself from so many people through fear, shame, feigned superiority, stupid jokes, sarcasm, cynicism, criticism, anger, arguing, talking behind people's backs, seeking out praise, clinging, sulking, and searching for pity. All the thoughts of shame and anger that I'd cultivated through childhood were concentrated and repeated intensely from 1982 onwards until the chemical balance in my brain was completely skewed.

The cause of my depression was anything but simple. But for years I blamed the wrong issue, which delayed me from climbing my mountain.

It might be simpler for you. Or it might not be. Just don't assume you know the cause of *your* depression because being wrong about it can delay and stymie your climb up your mountain.

> Depression isn't a disease; depression is a normal response to abnormal life experiences.
>
> — Johann Hari

(Hari, 2018)

> When you keep criticizing, judging, or shaming your kids, they don't stop loving you, they stop loving themselves.
>
> — Anonymous

Accept your feelings

No doubt you have very strong negative feelings about yourself, your depression, the events that led to your depression, and even the people involved in those events. Strive to accept your feelings, without judgment. They are what they are. Being open and honest about them is a starting point for shifting your mindset. It's okay to feel down or upset. There is no such thing as a "wrong" emotion. An emotion is an emotion. It's what you *do* about that emotion that counts. Once you accept your feelings without shame or blame, you can begin moving forward.

Do one thing

I know you want everything solved and the burden removed right now, but you climb a mountain one step at a time. Each step is a small win.

You won't climb anything by lying in bed or sitting on the couch. I totally get that your desire to get up and do something is frequently non-existent. Your mind has you convinced that there's no point, that you should avoid everybody, and that you should give up. If you don't change the station and break up that isolation, you risk getting stuck in a loop of negative thoughts that pile up until you feel like you can't take it any longer. It's an awful catch-22 situation where you know you have to do something different but feel convinced that you can't do anything or that whatever you try will be unsuccessful.

Where do you start to break that kind of thinking? Keep it simple. Start with one thing: a walk around the block, drink more water, call a supporter, listen to an uplifting song, say yes to an invitation, buy some vegetables. Just one thing. There are more things you can do later in this book.

Take one step up your mountain. You won't conquer the mountain with that step, but you will show that your mind is stronger than you think and you will have something positive to celebrate. Doing the small things over and over is how you climb the mountain.

Shift your paradigm to change your self-beliefs

We don't draw into our lives what we want; we draw into our lives what we believe.

The quality of your life mirrors the quality of your beliefs. What you believe about yourself is what you get. That's true for depression and true for life generally. The kind of energy you put out comes back to you. If you tell yourself nobody understands, or nobody can help, or that it's all hopeless, you're right every time, aren't you? You're not jinxed. Belief is what does it.

It's a choice to change what you believe about yourself and not be ruled by depression. I'm not saying you're to blame for having depression. I'm saying that you must make a choice about how you approach it. *You* must do it. Nobody will hand you a solution.

Depression is definitely an illness, a problem. But it doesn't have to be a permanent disability that you're stuck with. It feels like a disability because you've trained yourself to think that way. Depression doesn't arise like cancer or diabetes. It doesn't even arise because of events that happen in your life. It takes hold because of *beliefs* you hold about yourself in response to those events. The chemical imbalances of depression are responses to your beliefs and emotions. That means your beliefs control your depression.

Changing your beliefs requires work. Work that is well worth it. Talk to your mental health professional about some tools for changing what you believe about yourself.

When you're depressed, you believe negative things as if they're facts: that you're unworthy, that you're alone, that nobody cares, that you're unlovable, that you suck, that you screw up all the time, that you deserve bad things, that everyone else is an asshole, that there's no point trying, that things will keep going wrong, and that you expect shit to happen to you. Then those negative things come true and you say, "I knew it. That's just typical." These beliefs are so powerful that they cause a chemical change in your brain, which has a profound impact on your well-being, physically and psychologically. And they can feel unshakeable. It's a vicious cycle. Bad things happen, prompting you to believe negative ideas, causing and worsening your depression, making more bad things happen, and thus keeping you believing negative ideas and having negative experiences. I remember many depressive episodes where I thought, "This is my lot… Nothing will get better… I'm stuck with depression for life... I suck... What's the point?" Guess what happened? My depression persisted and things went wrong.

Turning depression around requires turning around your beliefs – and having plenty of help and support to do so. Beliefs are not wishes or hopes. You can't wish depression away nor "cure" it with the snap of your fingers. You have to work to change what you believe deep down in your core. You are the creator of your reality. You can't change what has happened. But you *can* change your beliefs.

> Between stimulus and response there is a space. In that space is our power to choose our response. In our response lies our growth and our freedom.
>
> — attributed to Viktor E. Frankl, Holocaust survivor

Perhaps right now you're thinking this is that "positive thinking" crock of shit again. No doubt you've seen those "glass is half full" positive thinkers who tell you how great it is and you want to tear their eyes out. Everything seems to go their way. You tell yourself that their positive attitude works for them, but can't ever work for you. That's because you don't believe it. Maybe you've tried telling yourself positive things and nothing changed. Maybe things even got worse and you wanted to give up. It's because you still believed the negative stuff. You were still convinced. The positive thoughts conflicted with the beliefs that you cling to at the deepest level. I'm not blaming you here. It was exactly the same for me, because I still believed I was a bag of crap. I lost count of the times I had a depressive episode and yelled out that all the work, help, and treatment for my depression had been bullshit, that I felt cheated, and that I was back to square one in the doldrums.

Persist. You *can* change your beliefs. It just takes time, repetition, and persistence. One or two therapy sessions will not undo months or years of depression. A few positive thoughts on their own won't turn things around. But they represent a step up the mountain. Therapy and positive thoughts over weeks, months, and years can definitely make a big difference. Your depression beliefs became entrenched through time and repetition, so it stands to reason that your journey to a better place should follow a similar pattern. As I write this, I've been working at changing my beliefs for five years. I'm still at it. It's a process. As some old TV commercials for Pantene shampoo said: "It won't happen overnight, but it *will* happen."

I encourage you to write this down and put it in a place where you will see it every day:

I can change my future. I can choose my destiny.
I can live with depression or I can take steps every day to grow and change. It's a journey that I must continue for life.

You'll do more work on this during your climb up the mountain.

Accept help

You don't have to climb this mountain alone. Every time a person offers help and support, take them up on it. There is no shame in doing this. On the contrary, it's smart. You are opening yourself to new ideas and perspectives. You are inviting goodness and love to where they have been lacking. You are letting the strength of others feed you.

Celebrate, be grateful

Not every day with depression is the worst. Some days you bounce back a bit, or perhaps some good things happen. But on those days, you might not acknowledge any momentary improvements. Instead, you may feel shame about being so down on other days, or you may cynically wait for the next bad thing to happen. This can cause you not to celebrate any occasion when you're "up" again, especially if you think celebrating will only end in disappointment when the next down day comes along.

You *need* to celebrate the good moments and be grateful for them. Without that little boost, the emotions of resentment and shame will maintain a powerful grip. Depression is built around resenting what has happened in the past and feeling ashamed of yourself in response. You can't go back and erase everything you feel resentful about, but you can steadily replace your resentment with gratitude. This is a key aspect of cognitive behavioral therapy for depression.

Sometimes it's very difficult to find things to be grateful for, especially if you're comparing yourself with the success of other people. So, start small and build from there. There's more about gratitude in "The climb" chapter.

FOUR

Choose a Sherpa

> There's no way around it: you NEED professional help for your depression and you need to put in the work.
>
> Sample an array of therapists and ask them about their methods and modalities for working through depression.
>
> If you can, go to each therapist a few times before deciding which one is best for you.
>
> Commit to the therapeutic process and work closely with a therapist for an extended period of time.
>
> Open your mind and do what you are asked to do.
>
> Do not expect to be handed a solution. When you are shown a pathway, only you can walk it.
>
> Fight through the pushback that tells you a therapist can't help.
>
> If money is tight, there are ways to still get help.

To climb Mount Everest, you need a Sherpa. There's no getting up there without one. A Sherpa is an expert guide who has been to the summit of Everest many times and has guided many other people there. This person knows the journey intimately – the landscape, the conditions, the pathways, the traps, the dangers, the risks, and the rewards.

For depression, your Sherpa is your mental health professional. It doesn't matter what title the person uses – therapist, counsellor, psychologist, psychiatrist, psychotherapist, cognitive behavioral therapy practitioner, and so on – as long as he/she is a clinical professional in the field.

Why this is essential

Working with an expert is the biggest and best help that you need for depression. When you're sick, you need a doctor. When you have depression, you need a therapist. Not only will your Sherpa know the kinds of challenges that lie ahead on the climb, he/she will come to know you, how you operate, and what your limits are. Best of all, your Sherpa will go with you on your climb, alongside you every step of the way.

Your mental health professional should help you address the *cause* of your depression as well as the symptoms. He/she should work with you to uncover the source of your suffering and explore ways to find some forgiveness and peace around it.

By the way, your Sherpa is not the boss. You are. Ultimately you are leading this climb. The therapist works for you and understands that you can fire him/her at any time. So don't look to this person to know, do, and provide everything. The one person who has the greatest power to improve your mental health is you. But to harness that power, you need a mentor and guide. Your mental health Sherpa is that mentor and guide, as well as a crucial companion, advisor, and supporter.

Dealing with pushback

If you've already been thinking, "Oh, I went to a therapist. He was useless," or "They'll never understand me," then your depression is talking you out of it. Giving up and telling yourself that they all suck is what your depression wants. It's tricking you into making a bad choice and staying the way you are. If you had a poor experience with a therapist, try somebody else. Whatever happened before is not a prediction of your future.

You are *not* alone and you are *not* the first person to have depression. The experts **do** know how to help. Depression *is* understood and can be helped, provided you are willing. So *commit* to doing the work with a clinical professional. If you're not making progress with one therapist, it's either that you don't want to change badly enough (you just want the pain taken away, which is totally understandable) or you stopped doing the work too soon.

When you work with a professional, your depression will continue to fight you. Be prepared for that. That may be why you thought therapists were no good. Don't expect to be given a cure or solution. Have no expectations at all. Just have the desire to learn, to change, and to work at it.

> Were therapists required by 'truth in advertising' legislation to tell their reality, then virtually no one would enter therapy... It is your defenses, not your wound, that cause the problem and arrest your journey. But removing those defenses will oblige you to feel all the pain of that wound again... You will not be spared pain, vouchsafed wisdom or granted exemption from future suffering... Therapy will not heal you, make your problems go away or make your life work out. It will, quite simply, make your life more interesting.
>
> — James Hollis

(Hollis J. , 2001)

The Sherpa knows what the mountain's summit represents

You've never been to the summit, so you don't know what it's like or about. Your Sherpa does.

You weren't born with depression. Something happened that caused it to take root. After all this time of being in pain, you are no doubt desperate for some relief. Sure, easing a few symptoms is nice, temporarily. But pruning the branches of a tree is not the change you need. The roots have to be dug out.

Going to the summit of the mountain means going to the very cause of your depression. Your mental health professional can guide you through how to identify the cause and how to release the thoughts and beliefs you're clinging to around it. It will take time and it will be very, very challenging. I needed a couple of years of work and support just to get through the resistance in my mind. I admit freely it was extraordinarily hard work and I had many episodes where I broke down screaming and crying. But I kept at it because for too long the mountain had dominated my life. So, open your mind, especially to things that hurt or cause strong reactions, because those things need to be healed.

Let your guide take you to the cause. Then you'll have a chance to change your life for the better.

If you can't afford one

If your budget doesn't stretch far enough to hire a therapist or a doctor, or you don't have health benefits, there are other options. Try your local community centre, university, college, hospital, school, or place of worship. Some counselling services receive government assistance for people who cannot afford full fees and thus can offer discounted rates. Check your employee assistance program or contact a mental health organization and ask what resources are in your area. Even ask relatives and friends for financial support or launch a crowdfunding campaign. If you truly want help, you will find it.

Lose the stigma and expectations

Many people feel a great stigma or shame about seeing a therapist, especially men who have been brought up to be "tough" and believe that talking about feelings and mental health is "weak". But we're in the 21st century now. There is great awareness about the importance of mental health and enormous support for people seeking help.

So, let's be clear. Counselling is *not* weak or shameful. It is smart and sensible. There is no difference between seeing a doctor for physical health issues and seeing a therapist for mental health issues.

Counselling is *not* about judging, imposing values, or giving you solutions.

Counselling *is* about exploring difficulties, listening, helping you understand why you feel the way you do, searching for helpful pathways, encouraging new perspectives, and providing tools. Counselling is also private and confidential.

During counselling, you will be encouraged to retrain your thought patterns to recognize triggers, develop strategies, reduce the power of shame, and live more in the moment rather than be paralyzed by shame about the past or anxiety about the future.

In the end, therapy is for you, nobody else. Just go. You're worth it.

Choosing a Sherpa

There is no "one size fits all" when it comes to therapists. Not every expert is for everyone. You should try out a few, especially if you've never seen one before. Some are more empathic, while others can be challenging, even confrontational. Some therapists use a transpersonal approach, some use cognitive behavioral therapy, some specialize in eye movement desensitization and reprocessing (EMDR), some follow the approach of legendary psychotherapist Carl Jung, some follow a Rogerian "common ground" approach, and so on. One or two of these approaches might work with you, while others may blow up. Therefore, go to a therapist a few times before being certain that that professional is right for you, or not.

It's easy to be confused by titles, credentials, and letters after a therapist's name, so here is a very basic guide.

- A **psychiatrist** is also a medical doctor who can examine you from multiple perspectives: biological issues, psychological issues, trauma, family history, substance abuse, addiction, and much more. In most countries, only psychiatrists and other medical doctors can prescribe antidepressant medication.
- If you want a **psychologist**, look for a clinical psychologist, as opposed to a research psychologist. A registered clinical psychologist will have at least a Master's degree in their field and

will examine how you think, feel, and behave from a scientific perspective in a bid to help you change your behaviour. Many psychologists specialize as social workers, marriage therapists, or family therapists, as well as clinical therapists.

- **Psychotherapists and other counsellors** can be very diverse in their fields and approaches. Some may even use creative methods like visual, dramatic or musical arts to assist people who struggle to articulate their feelings. While many jurisdictions do not require psychotherapists to be licensed, it would be wise to choose somebody who is a member of a credible professional organization and is insured to offer therapy services.

Look for a therapist you feel safe with and who makes it okay for you to say what you feel. In other words, look for someone who is part of your "tribe". In your tribe, there is safety, security, support, and connection. Most importantly, there is trust. The famous psychologist Carl Rogers essentially said that the relationship is the therapy. The idea is to have a safe space where you, the patient, can "re-parent" yourself.

Open your mind. The person you hire might have an unusual way to open a door or to raise your consciousness and show you something you've never seen.

Last, choose somebody who challenges you to continue working outside your sessions. You cannot rely on therapy sessions alone to do the job.

What if my Sherpa isn't right for me?

There are occasions when a climber needs to change Sherpa guides. Before you change, perhaps discuss it with your supporters. Their input could be vital. Just be sure you change for a good reason, such as needing to feel safe, secure, and connected. It's not okay to change Sherpas just because you are challenged. The climb up your mountain is supposed to have moments of challenge and discomfort.

With a new Sherpa, you might feel like you're beginning the climb again from scratch, but you're not. You have still learned from the first Sherpa, gained more understanding about what you are capable of, and have had a taste of what the climb is going to be like.

Personally, I changed psychologists after about five sessions with one. That first Sherpa was good but he and I didn't speak the same "language" and I felt the approaches were not direct enough for me. When I met a second psychologist, I knew in five minutes that she was the right choice. Her compassionate approach was so unusual and nothing like I expected. She challenged me directly, in an encouraging way, and set me homework to do. She showed me I didn't have to fear the climb, I just had to do the work. Even though she was a registered psychologist, she came across more like a mystic. That approach had not appealed much to me in the past, but I was intrigued. So, I trusted her. After we unlocked the cause of my depression, it was she who let me go, with the advice to call her again if I experienced difficulties or needed her help. Her trust and faith in me inspired me to work on re-programming my mind every day.

FIVE

Assemble your team

Enlist companions, helpers, supporters, in addition to mental health professionals.

Tell them what you're doing and ask them to support you with honesty.

Accept their help and support, even when it challenges you.

Nobody has ever climbed Mount Everest alone. Likewise, nobody has ever overcome depression alone. Both are a team effort.

To tackle your depression, you need a team of people around you to help you and support you. There will be times in your climb up your mountain when you'll feel stuck at the bottom or trapped on a cliff. In those moments, you need somebody beside you to say, "I'm not giving up on you! I believe in you! Come on, let's take this next step!"

Maybe a voice in your head says you have nobody or that nobody cares or understands. It's bullshit! Depression isolates you and grows in power by convincing you that you're alone.

> Have you ever heard of someone going into a psychologist's office and saying, 'I truly feel loved, appreciated, and respected by my friends, family members, and coworkers, and I am depressed'? Depression is an understandable default reaction for anyone who does not want to deal with the stresses and pressures of modern life, who feels alienated, unconnected, disconnected, poorly connected, unloved, and possibly unlovable.
>
> — Ira Israel

(Israel, 2017)

Reach out and ask for help. It feels scary, but it's a smart choice to make. There's no way anyone will just turn up out of the blue and start helping you.

Your team will be made up of family, friends, and loved ones. Look to the people who have said they'll support you in any way they can. Contact those who have said, "I'm here for you," or "If you need anything, call me." Take them up on it! Your depression will tell you to reject their offers, trying to convince you that they can't really help, that you're just burdening these people, and that it's somehow more "noble" to carry on alone. Get past any feeling of guilt or shame and accept support. One of the key elements that has made 12-step therapy programs so successful is that the patient admits they are struggling alone with their problem and need help.

Ensure your core team is comprised predominantly of people you can talk to in person or by phone, not just via text or social media. In fact, I recommend not looking for support via social media or other electronic platforms because they are grossly inadequate compared with the real human interaction, love, and support you need. Wrote Ira Israel, "One hug equals one million Facebook likes." (Israel, 2017)

Some of your team will go alongside you as you climb your mountain, motivating you to keep going. Others will be part of your base camp, either at home or available to contact when you need it.

Your team cannot climb the mountain for you, nor should they try. What these people *can* do is help you stay on track and assist with the training, tools, and supplies that you need for the climb. They can help you carry the load so you can climb higher. They can even provide a push when you really need it, even if you pretend you don't need it.

Turn to them as you climb. Trust them. Lean on them sometimes. Accept and receive their help and support. Don't be defensive or shut out helpers. Allow love to be exchanged.

You are never alone. See mental health professionals. Tell your friends. Join support groups. Reach out. Ask for help. Ask and you will receive – provided you really want to change.

SIX

Train

> **Help yourself prepare to climb the mountain:**
>
> - Be physically active in some way every day.
> - Be in nature and natural light.
> - Eat better.
> - Consume less sugar.
> - Drink more water.
> - Cut down on alcohol and drugs.

Climbing the tallest mountain in the world requires preparing and getting into better shape, both physically and mentally. The same goes for tackling depression.

Move and exercise

Exercise improves mood and state of mind. That is supported by a vast array of scientific research and is not disputed. For instance, the Mayo Clinic declared that "research on depression, anxiety and exercise shows that the psychological and physical benefits of exercise can also help improve mood and reduce anxiety" by releasing endorphins, taking the mind off worries, improving confidence, and providing a healthy coping mechanism. (Staff, 2017) Furthermore, a 2019 study involving more than 17,000 people with depressive symptoms showed that meeting guidelines for both moderate-to-vigorous aerobic physical activity *and* muscle strengthening exercise "was associated with a lowest likelihood of reporting depressive symptoms". (Bennie, Teychenne, De Cocker, & Biddle, 2019) There are so many more research materials out there demonstrating the positive effects of exercise on depression.

Exercising is one of the most important things you can do to help you climb your mountain. So, make it a priority every day. For too long you've allowed other things to be priority, including negative thoughts and beliefs. For instance, you don't need to check social media first thing every morning. Why feed yourself negativity, jealousy, cynicism, shame, and outrage? Why not move your body? You and your health are more important than social media.

Now, I know you don't feel like it. Depression wants you to be sedentary, convincing you that you can't get off the couch or get out of bed. It's not that you can't, it's that it *feels* easier to do nothing. And right there is where circular thinking can take over: it feels easier and less painful to stay down, yet being inactive increases depression's hold and keeps you down, so you feel guilty or ashamed for not exercising, making it feel easier again to do nothing. This vicious cycle makes you less motivated, thus keeping you down longer, thus feeding your guilt, and creating this belief that you're trapped and incapable of doing anything at all. But you are not to blame. You are not a loser or a failure. It's not a question of character. It's merely a symptom of depression.

Therefore, pretty much the only thing to do is… do something. Don't wait for motivation. It won't come. The longer you stay still and wallow in depressive thoughts, the stronger depression's hold over you will be. And don't make elaborate plans. That will delay you and reduce your enthusiasm. Do something within five seconds of thinking of it, otherwise your brain will invent excuses and convince you not to do it. Make your plans *after* exercising.

Strive to do something every day. Do anything. The good news is that you don't have to get in mountaineering shape. You don't have to run a half marathon or do P90X. Even a light stroll in the fresh air can alter your perspective. You can move. You can. Then congratulate and thank yourself that you did it.

And don't beat yourself up with shame if you have a day here and there where you can't.

By the way, if you battle anxiety along with depression, exercise helps here, too. With anxiety, you release a ton of adrenaline each day that doesn't get used properly. Basically, your body goes into "fight or flight" mode a lot. When that adrenaline isn't used up in a positive way, you crash and feel very low. Exercising helps dissipate adrenaline more effectively.

Be in nature

Fresh air and moving around in the outdoors are huge for mental wellbeing. So is being in natural light.

I know it's easier to stay inside where it feels "safe", but it's not helpful for your depression. Being in the outside air *is* helpful. Train yourself to focus on breathing that air and on the sense of freedom you can experience for a few moments out there. The journey to break the continuous grip of darkness could begin with one small moment of light and air. Then another. And another.

Eat better

Poor nutrition, fast food, heavily processed food, masses of starchy carbohydrates, and excessive sugar all reduce your physical energy, wreak havoc on your bodily systems, and negatively affect your mental patterns and mood.

It's very simple. Eat clean more often. Cook whole foods at home more, eat out and take out less. And have vegetables dominate your plate.

Consume less sugar

The link between consuming too much sugar and mental health problems is very clear. Excess sugar disrupts the balance of brain chemicals and hormones. Unfortunately, sugar is added to almost everything in the western diet, often hidden under different names. It's especially prominent in comfort foods we turn to when depressed and stressed. Find ways to have less of it.

Drink more water

Plain water. Be better hydrated and cleansed. It's that simple.

Cut down on alcohol and drugs

People with depression frequently use alcohol and other drugs to mask or numb their mental pain. Used in large, regular quantities, these substances don't help at all, but rather make depression worse and harder to overcome.

Now, if you've read some research that says a glass of wine each day helps mental or physical health, fair enough, but that doesn't mean more is better. An occasional drink is no big deal. Just avoid bingeing or using it as a crutch, because what goes up must come down – with a crash. Moderation is good. If you're taking antidepressant medication, please follow the advice of its label and the advice of your prescribing doctor.

Meanwhile, stay away from addictive recreational and prescription drugs. That includes cannabis, which can help with several problems, but not depression.

It doesn't matter how much you love the feeling of getting drunk or getting high and escaping from the noise in your head. That pain will be there when you recover. In fact, it will come back worse. The crap you consumed will have a negative effect on you, making you want to consume more alcohol, more drugs, and potentially sending you into a spiral.

If you are dependent or addicted, find a rehab program and sign up immediately. Don't go it alone. Get professional help and social support, just like with depression. You *can* get out of the spiral, provided you truly want to and provided you take action.

SEVEN

Gather equipment and supplies

- **Medication. If it is prescribed for your depression, take it.**
- **Adjust your diet.**
- **Allow love into your life.**
- **Set up the lines of communication with your support team.**
- **Learn from other climbers.**
- **Choose mentors and read or listen to their materials, books, videos, podcasts, etc.**

There are specific tools and equipment you will need for your climb up the mountain.

Medication

If you are prescribed antidepressant medication, please take it. It can be a hugely important tool on your climb. Depression involves a chemical imbalance in the brain, and sometimes there can be no positive progress until that imbalance is addressed.

Medication can *help*. It's not a cure or solution, so don't expect it to be. It's a tool that can help ease symptoms and bring them under control so you can tackle the main issue: the cause of your depression. The chemical imbalance in your brain is the result of trauma coupled with negative thoughts and beliefs. It makes sense to address these chemical issues to clear the way for addressing the beliefs. Medication is one piece of the great puzzle, one tool in your backpack. Use it in conjunction with all the other tools, as part of a comprehensive plan to climb your mountain.

Antidepressant medication won't make you feel instantly better. It takes time for the effects to accumulate. The idea is to stabilize you, ease your worst symptoms, and gradually make you feel a little more like yourself. After a few weeks of medication, you may not feel like a dramatic shift has occurred, but you should notice yourself coping with some situations better than you might have a few weeks earlier.

Never be your own doctor. Please take your medication exactly as prescribed. Ceasing medication without professional supervision can be dangerous and very unpleasant. If the medication you take is not ideal or has unpleasant effects, talk to your doctor. There may be other options. You must discuss any changes to your medication program with your prescribing professional who has been trained formally and extensively. If you want to use, say, herbal approaches or something else that's not pharmaceutical, again talk to your doctor. As long as the other treatments don't interfere with the medication or your treatment, they'll probably agree.

And don't listen to any of that talk about "Big Pharma" profiting. This defeatist approach can feed your depression with thoughts about nobody being able to help. It can even set you up to isolate yourself even more by believing a conspiracy and thinking you know something many others don't.

There is no shame in using medication to assist you on your climb. If it helps, use it. That's just being smart.

Diet

To climb the mountain, you need the right supplies. When you consume too much processed food, junk food, deep fried food, carb-heavy food, and sugary food, you're not supplying yourself with the nutrition you need to climb the mountain. In fact, you're consuming stuff that will diminish mental sharpness, cloud your judgment, and make your body tired and not work properly. That goes double if you're regularly drinking alcohol. Furthermore, consuming these kinds of foods and drinks for comfort can send you into a cycle of feeling ashamed, then consuming more to comfort yourself, then feeling ashamed again, and so on.

You don't have to become a nutrition freak. It's very simple. Less sugar, less processed food and beverages, less junk food, less alcohol. More whole foods, more fresh vegetables, more fresh fruit, more lean proteins, more healthy fats.

And more water. Drink plenty of plain water to help your body and brain function properly.

Oxygen/love

Climbing Mount Everest requires carrying oxygen with you. When you're fighting depression, the oxygen you need is love – the love and support of others and the love you can give yourself. You need that love desperately. And crucially, you must be open to receiving it. Many climbers high up on Mount Everest suffer oxygen deprivation and don't know it, which negatively affects their decision making and skews their sense of reality. It's the same with depression if you don't understand that you're lacking love. If you attempt the climb without love around you, without giving and receiving it, you will be unable to withstand the challenges and will turn back.

One of the major causal factors in depression, and a factor that worsens it, is the withdrawal of love. It can feel like love gets cut off or withdrawn through trauma, betrayal, anger, abuse, punishment, the end of a relationship, death, illness, injury, parental response, etc. Even just the *feeling* of love being gone is enough for depression to be triggered or worsened, because withdrawal of love makes you think you are unworthy and undeserving. Then you feel ashamed or guilty, which is another way of withdrawing love. Before long, the victim questions come: "Why me? Why does everything go wrong for me? What did I do to deserve this?" In those moments, love is lost. You learn to hate everything around you, to hate yourself, and to believe that you attract or deserve shit. I mentioned illness and injury above because even these can make you experience a withdrawal of love. In the misery and pain of recovery, it's easy to feel powerless and cheated, like you've been given a raw deal.

In my case, I used the withdrawal of love as both a barrier and a weapon. It was at the very core of my depression. I grew up needing love. (What kid doesn't?) But I *felt* like at crucial moments love was withdrawn from me, leaving me feeling abandoned, scared, ashamed, and bitter. A key moment would have been when I was left to "cry it out" as a baby. Other moments included when I was disciplined (I was sent to my room and isolated), when I didn't live up to expectations, and when my family moved interstate in 1982. As a child, I didn't learn how to cope with a combination of rules, expectations, and feeling ashamed. Then, as I grew older, it didn't take much to trigger my old emotional memories and to reinforce the belief that I deserved shame and punishment, which of course I attracted. Over the years, to protect myself from being hurt again, I withdrew love from others. I withdrew myself and kept my distance – physically, geographically, and emotionally. For decades, if someone wronged me, I cut them out of my life, wrote them off, and held a grudge. But in using this approach to hurt others, I really hurt myself over and over, because I was essentially withdrawing love from myself. Even sitting in isolation during a depressive episode was self-punishment. (I was reliving being sent to my room.) Then I felt ashamed and guilty over it all, which made me withdraw and isolate even more, thus perpetuating my cycle of self-sabotage.

It took me years to understand that love was the oxygen I needed. Without it, depression remained firmly entrenched within me. Yet I was also scared to look for love and be vulnerable because I was scared it would be "taken away" again. I was stuck repeating the emotions I felt when I was a boy, and the withdrawal of love became a pattern. Through my teenage and adult years, when I received rejection from someone, I rejected them right back. "Fuck them! They don't know what they're missing. They can eat shit!"

I was 29 when my first marriage failed. My depression was truly dreadful for a couple of years after that. Without knowing it at the time, I relived all those old childhood emotions. Love had been taken away. "I must deserve it. I must suck. Why must I be dealt a shitty hand all the time? Fuck everyone, get them away from me!" Although I knew my marriage wasn't great in the months before the breakup, I was blindsided when the moment came. I had thought things would come good again. But there was nothing I could do and I descended into feeling like everything had been taken away.

A week or two after we split, I remember thinking that I didn't miss my then-wife personally. What I ached for was togetherness and intimacy, with somebody generally, not specifically her. *I needed love. It was my oxygen.* I'd always needed it, since I was a child.

When I began working with a psychologist years later, that was the moment I allowed love to return to where it was needed most.

That's a very brief summary of my loss of love (oxygen) at the heart of my depression. Love wasn't actually withdrawn when I was a child – my parents always loved me – but I *felt* like it was withdrawn and that's all that mattered because the feeling shaped my sense of reality. Love was what I needed most. It still is.

I'll take a safe bet that the withdrawal of love has played a big role in *your* depression. You need love back. You need that oxygen in order to get to the top of your mountain and change your life for the better.

> Going through anxiety or depression or any other psychological condition doesn't make you unlovable – it makes you human. And we love the person who trusts us enough to show us their humanity. Chances are there are people right now who are more willing to love you than you even know. Why not let them?
>
> — Seth J. Gillihan

(Gillihan, 2019)

> All obstacles that are perceived with love can be transformed into the greatest life lessons.
>
> — Gabby Bernstein

71

Communications

Real life mountain climbers use radios along with GPS and satphone technology to let people know their location, what they're experiencing, and how they're doing. Without such communications, these climbers can get lost.

Likewise, you must communicate with your base camp team to:

- Let them know where you are, what you're dealing with, and how you're doing.
- Reach out when things are tough.
- Stay in touch with others to keep perspective, stay grounded, and remind you of your place in the greater world.

Learn from other climbers

The pathways up the mountain are well trodden, so learn from those who have successfully summited and from those who have tried and failed.

> There are hundreds of paths up the mountain, all leading to the same place, so it doesn't matter which path you take. The only person wasting time is the one who runs around the mountain, telling everyone that his or her path is wrong.
>
> — Hindu Proverb

Mountaineers learn from each other all the time. They share experiences, tips, techniques, fears, triumphs, failures, and much more. By accumulating a body of knowledge, they make climbing the mountain a more manageable experience and increase their chances of success.

My path up the mountain may not be the same as yours. In this book, I mention many of the tools and approaches that have worked for me and my depression. You have to find the ones that work for *you*. And you do that by talking with other climbers.

First, there's your therapist, your Sherpa, who has been up and down the mountain alongside many climbers. This person knows an enormous amount about the terrain, the conditions, the pathways, what to expect, and how to succeed. A good therapist is two steps ahead of his/her patients… on a good day.

Next, talk to people who live with depression. You will see you are not alone like you thought you were. Listen to depression climbers who have either made the climb successfully or who have attempted it and failed several times. You can learn much from the struggles and failures of others, as well as from your own. As Yoda said, failure is the greatest teacher. Other climbers can show you some excellent techniques and tools for the climb. They can teach you much about the pathway up to the summit and what they encountered. You can build upon their work and step upon their shoulders to climb up yourself.

Next, research resources about overcoming depression, like this book.

Learn from mentors

Mentors are experts and inspirational leaders in the field of mental health. There are so many to choose from. Pick the ones whose style you like. Watch their video presentations, read their materials, check out their audiobooks and podcasts, and more. In the Helpful Resources chapter, I mention some publications that have been very helpful to me. I don't normally go for self-help books and speakers because, while they're well intentioned, I find many of them are wishy-washy, or they're preachy, or they're just full of peppy hyped up bullshit that tries too hard. After more than three decades with depression, I'd become so cynical that I thought the last thing I needed was a self-help book. I was wrong. If you feel the same kind of resistance, open your mind. Staying on the same old mental pathway will hold you in the depths of depression. Work with your mental health Sherpa to help adjust your thought patterns to be open to more ideas.

EIGHT

Establish base camp

You are about to tackle the most challenging part of your climb.
Therefore, you need a base camp.

When climbing Mount Everest, base camp is a safe staging area where you can prepare for the toughest part of the climb, and a shelter should storms or avalanches force you back down for a while. It marks a point that is as high as the regular climbing pathway can take you. Above that point is where the real climb begins alongside your expert Sherpa, for which you need ropes, picks, oxygen, and other special equipment for safety.

Base camp contains your support team, supplies, shelter, first aid, and communications. Your team will stay in touch at regular intervals throughout your climb, keeping you going and motivated. They can't climb for you, but they can encourage, cheer, offer advice, give love, believe in you, push you, and help lift you up when you're exhausted.

When tackling depression, your base camp may or may not be an actual place. Whether it be a physical or metaphorical location, there you will always have everything you need. Let your team members know you are working with your mental health professional. Ask them to stay in touch with you daily, especially after therapy sessions, and help you with life's needs like good food and warm hugs. Tell them each day what you are going through and feeling. The great thing is that, unlike on the real Mount Everest, you can see your base camp people at any time.

If your regular home is not safe or comfortable for you, ask reliable support people if you can stay at their places if and when you need. But be sure not to hide there. Base camp is not a place to hide. It is for preparing to climb the mountain, not for avoiding life or distracting yourself.

Have a vocation or hobby

Do something you are passionate about and don't try to earn money from. For almost everybody in our western culture, how they earn a living is very different from a vocation or hobby. Very few people earn a living doing what they truly love, which is okay, despite what some motivational speakers say. Many people who combine what they love with earning a living find that they start to lose some of the love and joy for the activity, precisely because the focus turns to making money. So, have something that is just for you, for the fun of it.

A hobby can be part of your base camp. It's something exclusively for you that helps keep things in perspective. Be sure it's something you enjoy that breaks up your day, helps you feel creative and productive, and gives you more social contact. Expressing creativity through a hobby shows, explores, and expresses who you are. You don't have to understand why you're passionate about staring at paintings or hiking or collecting stamps or dancing or bike riding or golfing or whatever. Do whatever is creative and constructive, whatever explores your passions, and whatever sends you down rabbit holes in pursuit of those passions.

Tidy up and be better organized

Clutter and mess are linked with anxiety and depression. So be sure your home and base camp are in good order. You don't have to become a neat freak. Just straighten things out around you. It will *help* your mind have some sense of order and peace.

NINE

The climb

The climb up the mountain is where you work to discover exactly why you have depression.

You will take many steps with your Sherpa guide, while using your equipment and relying on your support team.

As you climb, you will learn and apply many strategies to upgrade your mental "software". Most of all, you will learn a great deal about yourself.

Place no time limit on how long the climb will take.

Be prepared to feel uncomfortable and to experience pushback.

Do the "Own your life" exercise in this chapter.

Repeat the Forgive Mantra in this chapter and many other mantras multiple times each day.

Participate in support groups.

Meditate.

Practice gratitude.

Trust your Sherpa and the pathway, even if you can't see exactly where you're going.

Reduce the time you spend on your devices and on social media.

Keep taking one step after another.

> We know you're tired, tired and scared. Happens to everyone, okay? Just don't let your feet stop.
>
> — Haruki Murakami

The time has come. As long as you're prepared, it's time to climb towards the summit and learn what caused your depression. The climb takes place in therapy sessions with your Sherpa, in regular daily life with your support team, and even in moments of solitude when old thought patterns will challenge your resolve. Your job is to trust the climbing process and keep taking one step at a time. Have no expectations, just place one foot in front of the other.

During the climb up your mountain, you aim to:

1. Uncover the exact cause of your depression.
2. Understand that cause and how it has disconnected you from your true self.
3. Begin reprogramming your mind.

Figuring out the cause can be a big challenge. It requires exploring deep into your past to get to the heart of trapped negative emotions that have affected your self-belief and affected your brain's chemical balance.

As you climb, you must:

- continue working with your mental health Sherpa;
- check in regularly with your support team;
- open your mind to what your Sherpa is getting at; and
- do repetitive mental work inside and outside your sessions. A good therapist will set you work that you must do if you are to successfully examine your wounds, get to the core of those wounds, and begin healing.

Sometimes your Sherpa may take you up a pathway that you don't understand. You may even think it's the wrong pathway and that you're getting nowhere. Trust. Even if you don't fully understand, you're still moving upwards. At the very least, you're learning about the process of climbing and learning what the climb feels like. You're learning that you can do this.

How long will it take?

The climb up Mount Everest is a journey, not a race. Just keep working in the moment of now. Give it time, keep taking steps, and it will happen when it is supposed to.

Unlike on the real Everest, there is no specific timetable for you to conquer your depression mountain. When climbing Everest physically, an expedition must occur at a specific time of year (usually May), otherwise weather and the jet stream make it lethally dangerous. During the right climbing season, an assault on the summit must occur in clear weather and inside a strict time window. Outside that window and you must not attempt to reach the summit, otherwise it can be deadly as conditions, light, and weather work against you.

Fortunately, there are no such restrictions with your depression climb.

Meanwhile, never compare yourself with others and with their journeys. Have no expectations about how long it will take to get to the cause of your depression. It will take as long as is necessary and will happen when the time is right for you. (Refer to the "Own your life" exercise later in this chapter.) What matters is that you are climbing.

It will be uncomfortable

Climbing Everest has never been a walk in the park. Likewise, with depression, expect to be uncomfortable with what you face and what you experience. At times, this climb will be difficult and painful as emotions and memories come to the surface. Your Sherpa therapist will ask you to do things that make you look deep into your past and relive very unpleasant memories. Shame and anger and raw pain may come rushing up. Your resolve to continue will be tested.

Your depressed mind is going to push back and say, "No, I don't want to do this!... No, I can't do this!... Stay down! Everything is easier if I stay where I am... I don't have to do anything... I can just stay quiet and cover up, protected and safe." You may slip and stumble and become discouraged, thinking that you are going back to square one with depression. No, you aren't! Keep going! Your depression is trying to stop you from breaking through and taking control. Your depression does not want change; it wants to stay with what is familiar. You have felt this many times before and will feel great temptation to stop and give in to what feels familiar. But remember why you are climbing: to break the power these emotions have over you. Of course they will push back against change! That pushback is a sign you are doing something right. So, take the next step. Then the next. Staying still gets you nowhere. You must continue the repetitive work to release old hurts and reprogram your mind.

All climbers deal with this test, be they actual mountain climbers or people with depression.

Exercise

This is a great exercise for when you encounter uncomfortable emotions and triggers. It works even better if you have a trusted person read the directions for you.

Find a quiet place to sit. Close your eyes and breathe steadily and regularly for a few moments. Focus on your breath. If your mind wanders or keeps swirling, acknowledge that this is happening – without judging yourself – and return your attention to your breath.

Bring to mind a key moment from your past when you first felt depressed or that you associate strongly with your depression. See your younger self in that setting. Remember exactly how you were feeling and why. Now, in your mind, allow your current self to approach your past self and give you what you really needed at that time. Give your younger self the benefit of what you know now. Provide the support you truly needed back then. Allow the emotions to wash over you and through you. It's a very moving experience.

After this exercise, begin a daily practice of giving yourself the same thing(s). Allow yourself to receive the love and care and support that you needed back then – because you need it now.

Own your life

This exercise is from psychotherapist Ira Israel.

Find a mirror, look into your own eyes in the mirror, and say the following to yourself:

I am supposed to be me.

I am supposed to look exactly as I look.

My life is supposed to be exactly the way it is.

My childhood was supposed to transpire exactly as it transpired.

This act of "owning your life" — embracing every single moment that has transpired because every moment contributed to your being exactly who you are today — is a way to release all of your mind's resentments… "Owning" who we are, including our childhoods and everything that brought us to this present moment, simply means radically accepting reality and "giving up all hope of having a better past." And once we have stopped being victims of the stories our minds created, we can decide which daily tools — gratitude, loving relationships, helping others, healthy living, exercise, authentic communications, meditation, eating correctly, being in nature, and so on — will give us our adult version of "the good life."

(Israel, 2017)

Whereas pain is a physical experience, suffering is a mental one. It is the sense that things should be other than they are. Its antidote is acceptance.

— Wu Hsin

The Forgive Mantra

My psychologist gave me this amazing mantra to recite up to 200 times every day. I did. Its effect was (and is) nothing short of amazing.

I consider it essential for any climber. It's based on Ho'oponopono, the Hawaiian practice of forgiveness and reconciliation.

You might think the mantra is just words and won't change anything. I did at first. I was wrong. Be advised that these words can stir things up *big time* – sometimes in a challenging way, sometimes in a good way. Either way is important for making real progress up the mountain.

Try this mantra and see for yourself. Repeat it over and over every day.

FORGIVENESS MANTRA/PRAYER

In the blank space you can add one name or multiple names of people or situations. For example, names of family members, finances, job, relationships and so on. You can say all aspects of your health, job, finances, family, you name it.

Long Version of Mantra:
_____, please forgive me for anything I or anyone in the universe has done to create this situation in you, in us. Forgive me, forgive us. I love you. I forgive you. Thank you.

Read the passage 10-20 times placing your finger on each word. Placing your finger on each word helps encode or embed it into your subconscious mind. After that, start using the short version of the mantra where you can use the word FORGIVE as a substitution or code word for the entire passage.

For best results, use the short version at least 200 times per day while completing your chores, walking, or other daily activities. 200 repetitions takes approximately 15-20 minutes.

Repeating the mantra in your mind during a stressful situation is especially helpful for gaining mental clarity about the situation. It also prevents the stress from escalating. Using it throughout the day is the best approach as it helps break automatic, unconscious thought and behaviour patterns.

Short Version:
_____, forgive. I love you. I forgive you. Thank you.

Participate in support groups

I mentioned support groups briefly earlier. Try some out. There is strength in numbers. Withdrawing from the world never helps with depression.

There are many types and styles of support groups, not just one stereotype that you've seen in movies. For instance, a support group is not just a big downer where people grumble and complain. There are facilitated groups led by professionals (which include the very successful 12-step groups), there are open groups where things are more freeform, there are closed groups with defined memberships and times, and there are peer support groups led by people with direct experience. Release your expectations and try one. You have nothing to lose, while you stand to gain the knowledge that others are going through the same things as you and have different ways of looking at them. You also stand to gain new friendships. Listen, learn, unburden, connect. You may even find yourself wanting to help someone else.

What about online support groups? Perhaps one of these may help you a little, perhaps not. It comes down to your individual condition and how you respond. What matters most is that participating in online discussions inspires you to *take action*. If so, great. If not, try face-to-face support groups. On the positive side, online groups may help you feel more "anonymous" and safe when discussing your problems. Through such groups you may appreciate that you are not alone as you see others going through similar problems, and you may be encouraged to explore different approaches. On the negative side, there is no real in-person interaction, which only increases feelings of isolation; there is often a lot of negativity to absorb (people find it easier to unleash their worst feelings from behind a screen to an audience they can't see); and it's very easy to be pulled away into the vortex of online distractions.

> Depression is an understandable default reaction for anyone who does not want to deal with the stresses and pressures of modern life, who feels alienated, unconnected, disconnected, poorly con-

nected, unloved, and possibly unlovable. This is why transformational seminars, self-help books, and twelve-step meetings work: they teach people how to love or at least accept themselves and their lives, how to release their resentment at not being loved unconditionally, and how to feel heard without resorting to erecting egregious signposts such as alcoholism, debt, putative mental illness, physical illness, or other signals that people use when acting out in an effort to be heard by others.

— Ira Israel

(Israel, 2017)

Meditate

Okay, I can feel you cringing at the mere mention of meditation. I used to when people mentioned it. *Everybody* hates meditation until they don't. They hate it either because they struggle with it or because they think it's a load of crap. Even Dan Harris, the ABC news anchor and correspondent who is a meditation advocate, has written about a meditating friend of his "who jokes that when he considers the voice in his head, he feels like he's been kidnapped by the most boring person alive, who says the same baloney over and over." (Harris, Warren, & Adler, 2017)

If you're new to meditating, yes, it's difficult. But there are good reasons why so many people bang on about it incessantly. Meditation is simply about taking space to breathe and finding your true, authentic self in the stillness. (The negative depressive thoughts you experience in daily life do *not* come from your true, authentic self.) Extensive study has shown clinically that practicing meditation and mindfulness as part of cognitive behavioral therapy can significantly boost recovery from depression and that continued regular practice can help prevent depressive relapses. (Segal, Williams, & Teasdale, 2012)

If you still feel reluctant or think meditation is a bunch of hooey, read this list of other benefits you can gain from it and ask yourself if they are the sorts of things you would want in your life more regularly:

- Quieting your mind for a few minutes a day can go a long way towards handling depression, anxiety, difficult people, peer pressure, bullying, self-harm, and life's other obstacles with more peace and positivity.

- It's a way to feel centered again.
- Meditation is about bringing your thinking and your mind into the present moment. It is in the present moment where you can find some peace, focus, and clarity.
- Meditation enables you to briefly quiet the mental noise that says you cannot climb this mountain. When you find even a shred of mental peace, you discover how strong you truly are.
- Meditation is a crucial practice for reprogramming your mind. A few moments of calm can change the station that plays negative messages in your head all day.
- It can clear your mind so you can listen for your *true* voice. That true voice is small, quiet, comforting, loving, and will never steer you wrong.
- The psychologist Lawrence LeShan once attended a conference where, during a discussion among scientists who meditated readily, one described it as "like coming home". Overcoming depression, or even experiencing a few moments without its crushing weight, also feels like coming home.

Therefore, give meditation a go, multiple times. Yes, it might suck at first. You may struggle, it may feel clunky, your thoughts will likely continue to swirl, and you may question if it is worth it. But once you get a tiny taste of the nectar, you may start to understand and come back, much like hitting just one good golf shot out of hundreds can encourage you to keep playing. Even two seconds of your mind not torturing you can be inspiring. Ira Israel says when meditation works well, you go to the other side of your thoughts.

There is no one-size-fits-all with meditation. You don't have to do anything fancy or follow a religious practice. Meditation doesn't have to be about robes and essential oils and chimes, unless you want it to be, because that's okay. You can meditate any way you want, even by simply sitting and breathing. There are many kinds. Even the Forgive Mantra a few pages back can be a form of meditation.

If you have never meditated before or have struggled with it, start with baby steps. Try just one or two minutes a day before lengthening the sessions. And don't be angry at yourself if you don't last.

There are great guided meditations available free online, either through apps or on YouTube or other websites. They take you through how to relax, breathe, acknowledge thoughts that enter your head, and focus on peace for a short while. There are free guided meditations for any topic or situation. Most follow simple themes and practices such as breath awareness, body scanning, mindfulness, or loving kindness. If you are a religious person, you probably meditate without realizing it when you pray – therefore you could try transcendental meditation to rise above your mind. If you're an atheist, perhaps try some Buddhist meditations, since Buddha did not believe in a creator god and Buddhism is not a theistic religion. Some people who are more advanced with their practice can meditate while exercising, hiking, or doing yoga.

Look into experts who recommend and teach meditation. The psychologist Tara Brach offers Buddhist meditations. Or maybe try the founders of the Insight Meditation Society: Joseph Goldstein, Jack Cornfield, and Sharon Salzburg. Just look around, try different styles and practitioners, because there is bound to be something or someone that works for you. There's no formula, simply follow your tastes and decide what is most beneficial for you. It's possible your therapist could point you towards some good materials. My psychologist recorded a meditation personalized specifically for me that I would listen to each night as I settled down to sleep.

Set aside 5-15 minutes in your day, every day. You might say you don't have time for it, but consider this: if you're reading this book, you can spare a few moments for meditation. Remember, it's for you. Put your own health first. You cannot help others or do what they ask if you don't help yourself. You cannot pour from an empty cup. Looking after you is the most important thing you can do right now.

The best time to meditate is usually immediately after getting up in the morning. It sets a tone for your day. Another good time is as you settle into bed at night. Even if you fall asleep, guided mediation can seep into your subconscious and you might even sleep better. Just as long as you can be free from distractions and interruptions.

Perhaps one day during meditation you may glimpse the summit of your mountain.

Practice gratitude

Gratitude is a powerful force and the key to happiness. Every person you meet who is truly happy in life is someone who is regularly grateful for the things they have and experience.

What you put out to the universe is what comes back to you. The thoughts you think regularly will show up as your life. When you focus on negative thoughts, which come so easily when you have depression, more negative things keep happening. Similarly, when you regularly express thanks for good things, you train yourself to look for those good things and therefore you will likely find more and more of them.

Each day, try keeping a journal of three to five things that you're grateful for. Do that for two weeks and you should notice some slight improvements and changes.

Your depression will tell you that you have nothing to be thankful about or that you should downplay anything good that happens. It will try to convince you that the negative things outweigh the positives, and that there's no point trying. Pushing back against this mindset feels like such a big task, so stay away from the big things and start small and simple: "I woke up... I'm breathing... I got dressed... I ate breakfast..." and so on. These are all things to be grateful for, yet we've been conditioned to take them for granted. Each little win is worth celebrating, no matter how small or "trivial" you think it is. A win is a win.

Search throughout the day for more things you can be thankful for – clean air, food to eat, a bed, shelter, a pet, a friend, family, clothes, sunlight, air to breathe, a butterfly, you name it. Focus on those small things and become aware of how numerous they actually are. Just as you climb a mountain one small step at a time, saying thank you for small things creates an energy that can steadily attract more goodness.

It takes conscious effort to exercise gratitude regularly. And it's so worth it.

Keep it up, for life. Gratitude transforms lives.

Reduce social media time

When you're climbing a real mountain, getting distracted and thinking about another reality or location is unhelpful and dangerous. When you're climbing your depression mountain and working closely with your Sherpa, social media can be that reality-distorting distraction. On social media, it's easy to compare yourself with other people (and the image they have carefully cultivated for you to see), to search for outrage, to absorb cynicism and negativity, to feel drawn into justifying yourself, to ask for validation, to try to shame others, and to get sucked into debating, arguing, and point scoring. People post so much outrage online, often vicariously fighting back against who wronged them or what traumatized them. Such conditions are perfect for keeping you rooted in a cycle of depression, anger, and shame. Of course, there can be some positive aspects as well, but overall much of social media time is unnecessary and counteractive to your climb. Just watch the movie *The Social Dilemma* to understand how social media companies operate to make you addicted online – and keep you addicted – by employing artificial intelligence algorithms to use your own psychology against you.

These days I'm doing my imperfect best to scroll past outrage and to stay out of online debates, and I'm happier for it. I strive to deal more with people around me and less with those in the ether. When I do interact with people via social media, I do it more with those close to me and less with people at a distance and people I haven't met.

Stay focused on what's important as you climb your mountain.

Search for the things that help you heal and feel love.

In fact, you can do more than just cut social media time…

Reduce device time

Nobody has ever overcome depression online. There is a clear link between excessive online activity and depression. Your devices take away real human interaction and make you more isolated and alone. Yet they overstimulate the dopamine response in your brain – the pleasure and reward chemical – causing you to come back again and again. So many of us scroll/play aimlessly on our devices all day long, instead of being in the real world and learning to love ourselves.

Have you ever noticed people take a device break and love it? There's a message there. Moderation. Balance. Variety. Perhaps it would help you to leave your device alone for a while and to stop using it to pass time and distract your brain.

By the way, texting or posting online is the worst way to talk to someone about what you're going through. It's far better to have a real conversation with a real person in the same room. Text takes away non-verbal communication, tone of voice, and physical touch. In other words, it takes away real human connection. "Mirror neurons do not fire via text message." (Israel, 2018) It's no surprise that depression rates have gone through the roof at the same time that using personal electronic devices has exploded. People are using text for communicating way too much and deluding themselves that it's real human contact.

Another disadvantage of trying to connect via text is being unable to "vibe" with somebody. Like a cat, some people benefit from simply sitting with a person, exchanging care and support without saying a word. But with text, there is an obligation to type continuously and maintain a conversation. Sometimes when conversation is difficult, just peeling an orange and sharing it in silence can say so much more.

Instead of typing a long conversation, use text to make a time to meet someone, ***then*** talk and/or just be together.

Put devices away before bed

Please do *not* take your phone or tablet or laptop to bed. Don't be a slave to it. Staring at a screen in bed can have an awful effect on sleep and mental wellbeing. The blue light from the screen disrupts how your brain makes melatonin for settling to sleep, as does the high-paced mental activity induced by late night screen time. You need to settle your mind, not fire it up.

Leave your device alone at least an hour before sleep. If you keep your device beside you when you sleep, you essentially decide to let your life be run by it.

TEN

Storms

As you near the summit, severe mental storms will be triggered. Be prepared for them.

The storms mean you're close to a breakthrough. A new reality is near. Storms can even transform you.

Keep working at the mental exercises and keep working with your Sherpa. Keep meditating. Keep communicating with your base camp support team. Do your best to ignore the temptation to "hide" or "numb yourself out".

The weather will be crucial to your success on Everest. You will find yourself frustrated by its power to make you or break you.

— from www.mounteverest.net

Why do you want to shut out of your life any uneasiness, any misery, any depression, since after all you don't know what work these conditions are doing inside you?

— Rainer Maria Rilke

(Rilke, 1929)

The weather and conditions near the summit of Mount Everest can change dramatically. So can your state of mind as you get closer to revealing the cause(s) of your depression. The mountain will not be conquered without a fight.

As you climb higher, you will experience storms, maybe even rock falls and avalanches. Waves of depression, fear, rage, shame, anxiety, apathy, and many other emotions will likely wash over you, sometimes wildly so. (They were very wild for me.) The storms and challenges can bring on many behaviours and emotions – shame, blame, conflict, self-harm, lashing out, isolation, hiding, avoidance, drug and alcohol binges, self-injury, suicidal thoughts, desolation, grieving, nostalgia, projecting, resisting change, and more. During my own storms, I fought intensely with my wife over some issues. It wasn't her fault, and her patience was tested to its limits. She was amazing. I directed a lot of my frustration and anger at her as a way of acting out and avoiding making peace with the people and issues at the heart of my depression – and as a way of avoiding making peace with myself.

These storms may make you want to revert to your old behaviours and patterns, like defending yourself vehemently and pushing people away. You may want to numb out like you have before, perhaps by drinking or doing drugs. The storms may feel so awful that you want to give up. But these storms are simply messengers telling you that you are close, and getting closer all the time. Your depression knows you are close and will fight back with everything it has. The storms are a sign that you are getting to the heart of the matter.

The intensity of storms are directly proportionate to the freedom and reward you stand to gain.

Because you know these storms will come, you can prepare and have strategies ready. Better yet, you can see them as vital signposts. This is because you are so close to being reborn into a new reality that you haven't imagined.

When you feel like the storms are too much, it's because there is something you cannot see or are refusing to see. Keep climbing, one step at a time, using your supplies and equipment. Giving up now can be devastating. Everyone who has attempted Everest and turned back due to bad weather has said it was gut wrenching to give up.

If necessary, shelter in place, wait out the storms, then continue.

Always continue. You've come so far.

The challenge of isolation

The higher you climb and the more resistance you encounter, the more you may feel alone and dwarfed by the enormity of the challenge. Other people cannot understand what you are going through on this part of the climb, except your Sherpa. In such isolation, your resolve will be tested to its limit. It is vital to stay in communication with your support team, no matter how far away they seem. Tell them what you are going through. Allow them to encourage you, nourish you, challenge you, cheer for you, and love you. They may not always say the things that you want to hear, but they want good things for you and to see you happy. Allow their good will to seep into your mind. Accept every piece of positivity they send your way. Being depressed for so long can cause you to reject compliments and love. Be open to receive them all, no matter how uncomfortable or vulnerable they make you feel.

Celebrate, be grateful

On the days when you recover from a storm and bounce back a bit, you may feel shame about being down. This can cause you not to celebrate being "up" again. But you need to celebrate and be grateful for the good moments. You got through the storm or challenge. You displayed resilience. You're still on the climb.

Otherwise, if you continually expect the darkness to return, what will happen? It will return.

Storms transform you

You know that the storms don't last forever. They always pass. Every storm you withstand does not make you weaker. On the contrary, it makes you stronger, more resilient, even more malleable. Just as physical storms shape the landscape, mental storms shape who you are. They transform you.

When a storm comes, it's okay to surrender to it. Let it happen and let it pass. Breathe. Open your heart, mind, and arms. The universe is trying to send you a message and create you anew. It is trying to show you a way of life and a version of yourself that you have forgotten – the real you and the life you should live. You cannot see it by hiding or by fighting. You can see it only by surrendering and allowing yourself to be transformed by the forces around you.

Depression is an amazing tool for transformation. We become crushed and dominated by depression because we resist, because we let fear and shame take over, and because we cling to old ways and hide. Transformation is hard. It's like birth. You are moving into a reality that you have no idea about and have never seen. Trust your Sherpa, trust your work, trust your process, trust your heart, and trust your soul. Surrender, be open, breathe, climb one step without thinking of the destination, and trust.

The life you didn't know you could live is getting closer.

ELEVEN

The Hillary Step

> **You have become sharply aware of why you have depression. Now comes the final push to release that cause.**

You break through the clouds and storms and see the last obstacle before the summit. The Hillary Step is a wall of ice and rock only 58 metres below the summit of Mount Everest. It's the most technically difficult part of the Everest climb and the last major challenge before reaching the top.*

At 8,790 metres, you're in a zone where you are totally exposed and your position is dangerously precarious. You are at your most vulnerable. The winds buffet you. Frostbite is a real danger. Breathing is essentially impossible without supplementary oxygen you brought with you. You can see the summit, or you at least know it is near. The only person with you is your Sherpa.

By this point, you know exactly why you have depression and how it developed. You're so close now. All that's left is to reach the summit and start releasing your old ways. (In my case, I realized I was at the Hillary Step in retrospect. I didn't know it at the time. All I knew was that it was very, very difficult.)

You know what to do. You must check your oxygen supply, feel the fear, and steel yourself for the final push.

Climbing the Hillary Step means taking some deep breaths from your oxygen supply, doing what you've prepared for and trained for, and reaching for the summit where you can finally forgive and let go.

When going for your summit, you will feel incredibly vulnerable. That's because you are. Exposing your deepest emotional issues and frailties is vulnerable and scary. But there is no courage without vulnerability, and vice versa. They are one. Being vulnerable means feeling at risk and being open to feel, even if it's unpleasant. Closing off feeling because it's difficult has caused you so many problems. When you are vulnerable, you feel almost naked against the elements. It's confronting and scary as hell. But is it weak? No way! Of course it's scary. You're opening up to and facing the very issue(s) that first put a heavy weight upon you and became your depression mountain.

Keep pushing on. You're about to do something you never thought possible.

* I am aware that the Hillary Step no longer exists because it was destroyed in a 2015 earthquake. But it had been an integral obstacle on Everest since Sir Edmund Hillary and Sherpa Tenzing Norgay first summited the mountain in 1953. Therefore, I found the metaphor entirely apt.

TWELVE

The summit

Reaching the summit means understanding exactly what caused your depression and starting to release its hold over you.

You may make several attempts to step on the summit. You may have several delays and setbacks. You still could be turned back temporarily by sudden storms or changes in conditions. That's because your depression hasn't stopped fighting and resisting the change you are bringing.

Unlike with Mount Everest, it's possible you may not actually be aware you are stepping up to your summit. You may feel as though you are still climbing like you have been for a long time. But these final few metres are the most confronting and most revealing, and they require professional guidance and monitoring.

Then, in the quiet of your reflections, you are there. Reaching the summit provides a view of the world and your life that you may never have experienced or expected. You may experience feelings of release, understanding, and profound emotion. Or you may feel relieved and drained. Don't expect to feel ecstasy or joy, although that's possible. Instead, expect to feel a weight lifted. Expect to see the cause of your depression in a clear, perhaps even simple, light. Expect there to be no judgment in this moment. Expect to reflect deeply on how far you've come and to understand that you are a good person and are not to blame.

It's very possible that you will understand and appreciate your summit some time after a session with your Sherpa. I did. Reaching the summit with my psychologist showed me what the jigsaw puzzle of my life should look like. But I still needed more time to complete the entire picture by connecting the other pieces of my past into it.

Be vulnerable and open

I mentioned that at the summit you will likely feel at your most vulnerable. This may be how you know you're actually at your summit. Your protective defences will be down and you will see the truth about your depression clearly. Good! Being truly vulnerable towards the cause of your depression is exactly what you have needed for a long, long time. Working through this is a very courageous thing to do and you should be proud. Remember the correlation between vulnerability and courage? One cannot exist without the other. Every courageous act in this life requires being vulnerable. Showing courage doesn't mean being tough. It means risking a lot; risking getting hurt.

Being so vulnerable can feel very frightening. That goes double for many men who, regrettably, are still told to this day that they should buck up, tough it out, and not be a pussy. Vulnerability has traditionally been difficult for men who have been taught to be stoic, tough, and "macho". But really, fear of being open and emotionally vulnerable comes to down to one thing: shame. Shame causes people to withdraw and become inauthentic out of fear of being hurt again. Key figures in people's lives can easily make them feel ashamed of who they are – and they are human beings who need love.

Every human being from birth needs love. Every baby is completely vulnerable and utterly dependent on love and care, which are provided through nurturing, touch, embraces, warmth, food, comfort, safety, security, communication, patience, understanding, and mentoring. When love is withdrawn through hurt, anger, inauthenticity, greed, jealousy, or spite, a baby becomes uncertain, anxious, and fearful. As the child grows, this translates into negative self-image, negative self-talk, and shame.

One thing never changes from infancy: the need for love. Every one of us needs it, for life. *Now* is the time to give and receive love so that healing and forgiveness may begin. With your old defences down, *allow* love in and out. Do as your heart guides you. Remember what it took to get here. Then continue your daily meditation and mantras, especially the Forgive Mantra.

It's okay to be vulnerable! It's a really important way forward for the rest of your new life. Vulnerability makes you open to be cleansed of the old and filled with the new.

> You don't really conquer a mountain, you conquer yourself. You overcome sickness and everything else – your pains, aches, fears – to reach the summit.
>
> — Jim Whittaker, first American to summit Everest

> Everest for me, and I believe for the world, is the physical and symbolic manifestation of overcoming odds to achieve a dream.
>
> — Tom Whittaker, first person to summit Everest with a physical disability

THIRTEEN

The climb down

> Keep learning to forgive. Forgive yourself as well as others.
>
> Your happiness ahead depends on letting go of past hurts.

Your journey isn't over yet. Reaching the top of the mountain isn't the end. Now you must get back down the mountain safely and return to regular life – a *new* life.

> I have climbed my mountain, but I must still live my life.
>
> — Sherpa Tenzing Norgay

You mustn't return to your old ways. You have seen and experienced too much. People who have successfully summited the physical Mount Everest have seen the world from a profoundly different view and have no chance of being the same people they were before their climb. If you revert to your old ways after the climb, you may not have truly stepped on the summit, or you may need to visit the summit again.

The climb down the mountain may be much less arduous than the climb up, or it may be just as challenging and risky. Either way, it requires you to continue doing the same things that enabled you to climb up.

As you descend, there may be some people who don't understand your climb or don't understand your new perspective. Those people could be linked to the cause of your depression and may not have changed. Nonetheless, you are starting a new life. What has changed is your perspective and your approach. You are learning to release and forgive, so that you can build a new and brighter future.

The power of forgiveness

It's time to learn what forgiving truly means and to experience it. It's time to come to terms with what has happened in your past. It's time to banish shame, guilt, and regret.

Forgiving does not mean approving of what happened in the past. It means releasing its power over you. Clinging to old hurts has kept you chained to depression for so long. Forgiveness is the pathway down your mountain and the pathway to your new life ahead.

The first part of forgiveness is to stop blaming others for your problems. The second part is to forgive yourself.

Perhaps you're not sure how to forgive. I certainly needed help with that. So did Fred Luskin, somebody far more learned than I. After struggling for years with being unforgiving, Luskin is now Director of the Stanford University Forgiveness Project. His work has shown that forgiveness is something you must develop as a skill in order to reclaim your personal power and wellbeing.

> The biggest obstacles to forgiveness, is that people have no idea what it is. They think that if they forgive, then they have to go home and have Thanksgiving with Dad who is horrendous. Or that if they forgive then they can't sue somebody. Or if they forgive that they are required to think that somebody did something that was OK. Those are all very different things.
>
> What it (forgiveness) means is that in your heart you are clean, and you are no longer blaming them for problems in your life. You are just choosing to release the bitterness that you have created in yourself, to just take care of your life.

(Luskin, 2017)

To learn to forgive, continue doing the work that got you to the summit of the mountain. Continue meditating, being grateful, exercising, eating well, using medication if it's prescribed, and so on. Keep reinforcing your new perspective, using your tools and equipment, and trusting your Sherpa. Especially keep repeating the Forgive Mantra again and again, day after day. Repeating those powerful words can help reshape how you respond to challenges by asking for love and by sending out love and gratitude. "Forgive. I love you. I forgive you. Thank you." Where once you had great difficulty letting go of hurts and wrongs, using this mantra on the journey down the mountain steadily makes releasing easier and easier.

Consciously start changing how you judge people, emotions, situations, and yourself. You are no doubt more aware now of how you have judged things and people before. Negative judgment caused you to cling onto trauma, hurt, and shame. Convert that judgment into the courageous vulnerability that is encapsulated in the Forgive Mantra. No doubt old ways of judging will enter your head. That's okay. Acknowledge them, breathe, and keep up the mantra.

And do the mantra on the days when you feel good, not just in challenging times. If you slack off on the climb down the mountain, there's a chance old depressive thought patterns that haven't yet been totally banished can creep back again. Shame and regret and anger must be released steadily over time; they can't be just dumped all at once, because they are deep inside at the most fundamental level.

It's possible that forgiveness might remain a confusing concept for a while. Don't expect it to be clear cut and simple. Expect it to be a journey and process with twists, turns, and doubts, just like climbing your mountain has been. You've made it this far, so you know you can do this.

> "What if I forgave myself?" I thought. "What if I forgave myself even though I'd done something I shouldn't have? What if I was a liar and a cheat and there was no excuse for what I'd done other than because it was what I wanted and needed to do? What if I was sorry, but if I could go back in time I wouldn't do anything differently than I had done? What if I'd actually wanted to fuck every one of those men? What if heroin taught me something? What if yes was the right answer instead of no? What if what

made me do all those things everyone thought I shouldn't have done was what also had got me here? What if I was never redeemed? What if I already was?"

— Cheryl Strayed

(Strayed, 2012)

Discover your purpose/vocation

Discovering your purpose and living it means never being imprisoned by depression again. This is a more advanced activity, for when you've summited your mountain.

To discover your purpose or vocation, pursue your passions. Use your gifts. Listen to the universe. Follow your bliss. If you love growing flowers, then grow flowers. If you love singing, then sing your heart out. If you love solving quadratic equations, then have at it. Whatever brings out your passion, because your love and passion will guide you.

If you follow your bliss, you put yourself on a kind of track that has been there all the while, waiting for you, and the life that you ought to be living is the one you are living. Wherever you are — if you are following your bliss, you are enjoying that refreshment, that life within you, all the time.

— Joseph Campbell

(Campbell, 1988)

You can tune into your passion, love, and desire when you are meditating, walking, exercising, or doing other activities.

I also recommend turning to mentors to look for your purpose. Read and listen to them. The book *Claim Your Power* by Mastin Kipp is great for this. Also wonderful is Ira Israel's book *How to Survive Your Childhood Now That You're an Adult* because he shows a clear pathway to become truly authentic in this world. As I write this, I have signed up for his online course with Udemy: "Authenticity and Awakening for Lovable Idiots".

Keep at it

Yes, I'm repeating something from earlier. Settle in for the long haul. This stuff must become your new normal. There is no quick fix. Depression does not get "cured" or banished overnight or in a couple of weeks. Expect to work on improving yourself and reprogramming your mind for a long time. Expect to do it for life. Look forward to doing it! If understanding, releasing, forgiving, and loving have helped your depression in any way, imagine what they can do for everything in your life ahead.

> You keep putting one foot in front of the other and then one day you look back and you've climbed a mountain.
>
> — Tom Hiddleston

FOURTEEN

What about the mountain now?

Well, it's not gone. The mountain is still there. It always will be. Climbing it doesn't mean levelling it nor wiping away the past. Now you see your mountain differently, with fresh eyes. Now you understand it. The mountain stands as a monument to your incredible journey and achievement. It remains as a reminder of what you had on top of you, what you climbed, and how far you've come.

You will always remember the worst of your depression. Those memories will never go away. But instead of being weighed down, shamed, and isolated by them, you will see them differently as well, and know that they no longer have a hold over you.

Now that mountain provides an amazing backdrop to your new pathway, your new journey, and your new life.

When you think about it, without depression, you may not have got to this incredible new place in your life. You certainly appreciate it more because of what you've been through in the past.

FIFTEEN

A new life

Every person who's successfully climbed Mount Everest has said it's a life-changing experience. It's the same when you get to the cause of your depression and start releasing it. Indeed, why would you look at life in the old way again? Why would you return to old patterns? Look how far you've come! Look back at how deflated, demotivated, defeated, and "lifeless" you were in the depths of your depression. Now look at what you've learned since then, at what you've done, and how your awareness and thinking are changing. That is truly awesome! How amazing you are! Take time to congratulate yourself and to celebrate your astonishing achievements on your climb.

Continue doing the things you've learned both before and during your climb. You know now that they are helping and transforming you. Keep at them. Keep retraining your mind. Keep working to change your beliefs about yourself.

Are you free from all storms forever after? Of course not. But you have weathered the worst storms of your life and been reshaped by them. You have learned how strong you are. Now you know how to handle any subsequent storms that hit. That climb up your mountain has been the most important thing you could ever do.

The power of love and belief

The biggest change brought about by your climb will be that love and joy have a chance to return to your life. Love is the answer, the root, the key. At the core of depression is negative self-belief triggered by the withdrawal, rejection, and blockage of love in some way, shape, or form. Every person on this planet needs unconditional love. Where love is missing, suffering takes its place.

While the cause of your depression may have made you believe love had been taken from you, the reality is that you blocked it from yourself and prevented it from flowing inside you. That's because, at that time, you didn't have the tools to understand and do something about the trauma that descended on you. Once you *believed* you were undeserving of love and blocked its flow for yourself, depression had taken hold. Depression persuaded you to seek out things that made you continue to feel poorly; things that made you feel shameful, unworthy, unloved, unlovable, isolated, disconnected, angry, envious, and unproductive.

Now you *do* have the tools you need.

No doubt reopening yourself to give and receive love felt scary and doomed to failure. It probably still feels scary. But the issue comes down to belief. If you believe being open to love will fail, it will fail. But likewise, if you believe love will help you, it will. And the way to believe is to repeat, repeat, repeat.

Love is everlasting, eternal, unbreakable, unchangeable. It can't be destroyed, only blocked or hidden. It is up to you to accept it, to feel it, to let it flow through you, to nurture it, and to exude it. In many ways it's like the Force in *Star Wars*, except it's not just for the chosen few. Everyone can become a Jedi.

If things aren't changing for you, it's because you're still clinging to what was, clinging to the hurt. You must accept what has happened, accept that it changed your life, and accept that it has even changed the world around you. (As I write this, the 2020 coronavirus pandemic has been raging for months. So many people are longing for what was, not accepting fully that things have changed.) When you accept what was, forgive it, release it, and accept what is new, only then can love and abundance flow freely and uninhibited.

Be open to receive

From now on, when people offer you support, allow yourself to receive it. That's being smart, not needy or dependent or weak. Allow yourself to receive help, advice, ideas, praise, compliments, favours, gifts, money, you name it. They nourish your growth. Receive them gratefully without putting yourself down or considering whether you "deserve" them. You are always worthy to receive goodness and love, but depression tricks you into thinking that you aren't. So, receive every gift without guilt, and be sure to celebrate *all* the good things that come to you, both big and small.

Pursue your gifts

Your gifts are what come easily to you and unleash your passion. Either your true gifts revealed themselves through your climb up and down the mountain or you are now free to look for them. Trust them. Use them.

Pay it forward

There's no need to repay the people who help you. (Except always pay your therapist's bill!) There's no obligation or guilt. They will be satisfied seeing you improve. Instead, pass on what you learn to others who need it. Give the love and support that you needed back when depression began descending on you.

A simple choice for everything in life

When your mind swirls with turmoil, doubt, negativity, and fear, instead of putting up your old blockages and excuses, remember that you have a choice. It's not a choice between doing something and doing nothing. It's the choice between *love* and *fear*.

Every time in your life when you must make a decision, the choice is the same: *love or fear*.

Which will you choose?

Meditate if you must, to quieten your mind and listen to the will of the universe.

Live bigger

Depression has made you live a small and constrained life for so long. When you return to your soul and put your faith in the energy of the universe, blockages will be cleared from your pathway.

As you have no doubt grasped by now, no one is coming to live your life for you. You must live it yourself. Do so by choosing to remain open to the universe's guidance. Imagine and dream your future life. Bring your unique gift. Make your mark. Celebrate love and life. Begin now. Make your life bigger and bolder. You took many risks to climb your mountain. Now you know you have the strength and courage to take many more risks. Everything you need is already within you.

SIXTEEN

The great reveal

In the "My climb and your climb" chapter, I wrote about deciding to change myself and then challenged you to change. In reality, as I worked with my Sherpa to climb my mountain, I didn't change me. I changed how I thought and how I looked at my depression. Instead of changing who I was, I *revealed* or *uncovered* who I truly am.

That's what really happens when you climb your mountain. You uncover your true self.

Me: Hey, Universe.

Universe: Hello.

Me: I'm falling apart. Can you put me back together?

Universe: I'd rather not.

Me: Why?

Universe: Because you aren't a puzzle.

Me: What about all of the pieces of my life that are falling down onto the ground?

Universe: Let them stay there for a while. They fell off for a reason. Take some time and decide if you need any of those pieces back.

Me: You don't understand! I'm breaking down!

Universe: No, *you* don't understand. You are breaking through. What you are feeling are just growing pains. You are shedding the things and the people in your life that are holding you back. You aren't falling apart. You are falling into place. Relax. Take some deep breaths and allow those things you don't need anymore to fall off you. Quit holding onto the pieces that don't fit you anymore. Let them fall off. Let them go.

Me: Once I start doing that, what will be left of me?

Universe: Only the very best pieces of you.

Me: I'm scared of changing.

Universe: I keep telling you - YOU AREN'T CHANGING! YOU ARE BECOMING!

Me: Becoming who?

Universe: Becoming who I created you to be! A person of light and love and charity and hope and courage and joy and mercy and grace and compassion. I made you for more than the shallow pieces you have decided to adorn yourself with that you cling to with such greed and fear. Let those things fall off you. I love you! Don't change, become! Become! Become who I made you to be. I'm going to keep telling you this until you remember it.

Me: There goes another piece.

Universe: Yep. Let it be.

Me: So, I'm not broken?

Universe: Of course not. But you are breaking like the dawn. It's a new day. Become.

— Author unknown

SEVENTEEN

Summary

This is a summary of a blog I wrote in 2019 outlining some tools and techniques you can use for depression and for your life after the climb.

If you've ever read *The Hitchhiker's Guide to the Galaxy*, you'll know that the answer to the great question of life, the universe, and everything is… 42!

Do these 42 things to climb your Mount Everest, to get back down, and to live your life afterwards. Over the course of time, do all 42 of them. If you don't, I believe you're not giving yourself a proper fighting chance to get on top of depression. Don't feel overwhelmed by there being 42. You can work on them a little at a time. Many of them you're probably doing already. And some are really simple.

You can do it. You can turn your life around and release the shackles of depression. If you want to.

1. **Do all of the things on this list.** Not just one or two, or three or four. All of them. Don't beat yourself up if you can't do anything some days. As P90X instructor Tony Horton said, "Do your best and forget the rest." Just do what you can, when you can.

2. **If you have thoughts of self-harm…** Contact a professional or a help line and talk about it. Immediately. You can. You'll never know how amazingly helpful they are until you call them.

3. **Want to change.** You must want to be different. Not just feel different or want the pain taken away. Everyone with depression wants those things. You have to want to change *you*. You need a strong desire to reprogram how you think. Nobody can do this for

you. People can provide guidance, but only you can make the changes. Until you honestly desire to be different, there is pretty much no chance of getting on top of your depression.

4. **Work with experts.** This is the biggest and best help that you need for depression. When you're sick, you need a doctor. When you have depression, you need a mental health professional. The experts *do* know how to help.

5. **Get help and support from loved ones and friends.** You need it. *Need.* Nobody overcomes depression on their own.

6. **Stick with it.** Stay the course. Keep working at making necessary changes. You will experience setbacks and episodes where you think you've gone back to square one. You'll have moments when you'll think all your work is for nothing. Keep at it. Reprogramming months or years of negative beliefs takes months or years. Pick yourself up, take another step. It's better than staying still or going back – because things really suck when you sit still on that old pathway you know so well.

7. **Lose the stigma.** There's nothing "wrong" or shameful about having depression. Nothing. The stigma comes from other people, not from you. You have depression. That's simply a fact. You are not diminished by admitting it and it doesn't define who you are. Get over any negative ideas and work on it.

8. **Depression is a symptom.** It's a symptom of a problem. It's not the problem itself.

9. **Depression is a messenger.** It's telling you that your old defence strategy is no longer serving you. Walls keep things out, but they also keep things in. If you don't change, the messenger will keep coming back and will get louder and louder.

10. **Stop depression tricking you.** "Depression is lying to you. Depression does not rob you of the choice. It just tricks you into making the wrong one." – Mel Robbins

11. **If you've been prescribed medication, take it.** Medication helps. It's not a cure, so don't expect that. Medication can help bring

symptoms under control and help you feel a little more normal. Use it in conjunction with all the other steps in this list. If you have any issues with it, never be your own doctor. Talk to your prescribing professional.

12. **Go deep to get to the cause.** Don't just prune the branches and let it grow again. Dig out the roots. You might think you know what caused your depression, but it's quite common to be mistaken here. Work with your mental health professional. It will take time and it will be challenging.

13. **Change your beliefs.** Depression is rooted in belief. Depression takes hold because of *beliefs* you hold about yourself *in response* to traumatic events. What you believe about yourself comes true. The chemical imbalances of depression are *responses* to your beliefs and emotions. Talk to your mental health professional about some tools for changing what you believe about yourself.

14. **Forgive yourself and others.** Forgiveness is the path to freedom. Forgiving doesn't mean approving of what happened to you. It means releasing its power over you.

15. **Reprogram with mantras.** Use the Forgive Mantra. Repeat other affirming and encouraging words to yourself. Your depression took hold due to negative thoughts repeating and repeating; you have to reprogram by repeating positive words. Give yourself love, honour, gratitude, confidence, and forgiveness. Over and over.

16. **Meditate.** It's the way to feel centered. Change the station playing in your head, even for just 10 minutes a day.

17. **Practice gratitude.** Gratitude is happiness. Every day keep a journal of three to five things that you're grateful for. Do that for two weeks and watch your situation change for the better.

18. **Exercise. Move.** Exercise helps mood and brain patterns. But depression wants you to be sedentary. The longer you stay sedentary and wallow in depressive thoughts, the stronger depression's hold over you will be. Don't wait for motivation. Do anything. You don't have to run a half marathon or do P90X. You can move. You

can.

19. **Be in nature.** Fresh air and moving around in the outdoors are huge for mental wellbeing. So is being in natural light.

20. **Eat better.** Poor nutrition, fast food, heavily processed food, and excessive sugar reduce your physical energy, wreak havoc on your bodily systems, and negatively affect your mental patterns and mood. Eat clean more often. Cook at home more, eat out less. And have vegetables dominate your diet.

21. **Consume less sugar.** Excess sugar disrupts the balance of brain chemicals and hormones. Sugar is included in almost everything in the western diet, often hidden in foods. Find ways to have less of it.

22. **Drink more water.**

23. **Cut down on booze and drugs.** Especially avoid bingeing, numbing, or using them as a crutch.

24. **Participate in support groups.** Connecting with others is crucial. Drop all your expectations and go. You will learn that others are going through the same things as you and might have different perspectives.

25. **Reduce screen time.** There is a clear link between excessive online activity and depression. Devices are addictive and take away real human interaction and make you more isolated and alone. Texting or posting on social media is the worst way to talk to someone about what you're going through. You need real conversation with a real person.

26. **Stay out of online arguments.** Arguing online achieves nothing. Nobody changes. But your depression can worsen because your arguing and "point scoring" is a way of acting out against who/what hurt you and triggered your depression. By debating online, you stay in a cycle of negativity. You'll only activate your triggers, your shame, and your depression messenger.

27. **Put your devices away before bed.** Leave them alone at least an hour before sleep. If you have your device beside you when you sleep, you choose to let your life be run by it.

28. **Turn off the news.** Or at least filter it. Spend less time on social media where people post news articles. 95% of it is negative news or provokes a negative response in you. You don't need that. The cycle of bad news sustains your stress and your gloom.

29. **Avoid negativity and cynicism.** Cynicism especially is everywhere on social media. People post cynical things because they identify with them. Whatever satisfaction or agreement you might feel from hearing/reading defeatist and cynical thoughts, you're more likely feeding your depression.

30. **Give and receive LOVE.** Love truly is the answer. And love for yourself comes first. How do you love yourself? Do the things in this list.

31. **Be vulnerable.** Remember that courage and vulnerability are the same. One cannot exist without the other. Yes, it feels risky, but it's the way forward.

32. **Be open to receive.** You are worthy to receive goodness and love. Depression makes you think the opposite. Receive with gratitude, not guilt.

33. **Have a hobby.** Something for you. Something you enjoy that breaks up your day, helps you feel creative and productive, and gives you more social contact.

34. **Tidy up and be better organized.** It will help your mind have a sense of order and peace.

35. **Accept your feelings.** There are no "wrong" emotions. Don't blame or shame yourself for feelings and emotions.

36. **Reach out.** Overcoming depression requires contact and support. Ask for help. Ask and you will receive.

37. **Learn from mentors.** Listen to them and read their materials.

38. **Discover your purpose.** Finding your purpose and living it means never being imprisoned by depression.

39. **Be patient and stay the course.** Yes, repeating something from earlier. Settle in for the long haul. There is no quick fix. Depression does not get "cured" overnight or in a couple of weeks. Expect to

work on improving yourself and "reprogramming" your mind for a long time. Look forward to doing it! It's a journey. It's a new way of life. Stay with it. You can.

40. **Act now.** Don't wait to feel "ready". It won't happen. Just get going. Do one thing now to help your depression.

41. **Pay it forward.** There's no need to repay the people who help you. There's no obligation or guilt. They will be satisfied seeing you improve. Instead, pass on what you learn to others who need it.

42. **Your choice for everything in life.** Love or fear. Every time you ever have to make a decision, it's the same choice.

EIGHTEEN

Supporting a sufferer

Supporting somebody dealing with depression is a challenge, to say the least. Thank you for being there! You are amazing! You are also appreciated, even if it doesn't seem so sometimes.

The big question for any supporter is: "What can I say or do to help and not make things worse?" Before we get into details, here are a few general guidelines:

- Be patient. Understand that you're not perfect and you're not supposed to be. Depression is a messy business and you'll make some mistakes. Many times you'll feel like there's nothing you can say or do to get through to the person and that everything seems to spark them off.
- Listen as much as you can. Don't try to solve.
- If the person lashes out at you, try not to take it personally. It's likely a symptom of a deeper problem.
- Understand that it's not the depressed person's fault. It's not your fault, either.
- Encourage. Offer support.
- Encourage the person to seek professional help. Just don't make that the first thing you say, in case it provokes a negative reaction or is interpreted as trying to palm the person off.
- Show that you won't give up on the person, even if they have given up on themselves. This can be very challenging if the person lashes out at you and makes you the target for their emotions. Remember that the person is expecting love and support to be withdrawn in a repeat of their original trauma and emotional wounds.
- Understand that the pattern of depression was set a long

time ago, so it will take time to change.

- You can't climb the mountain for this person. But you can climb alongside, or at least maintain basecamp.
- **Whatever you do, offer love. If it is refused or blocked, keep offering it. Love should guide all your words and actions.**

Don't let appearances fool you

Many people with depression are experts at hiding it. For instance, I was in a group that won an international singing championship, yet many people had no idea about my years with depression and were very surprised when I opened up. They'd seen me with the championship and with my family and thought I was happy.

When a person with depression appears successful, that doesn't necessarily mean they feel great and need no help. A person's happiness is not determined by success. Depression is always lurking, even during times when the person seems "fine". A good approach is to help the person celebrate the success and then work to build upon the positivity of the experience.

Foster communication, don't try to solve

Your words can't solve depression, so don't approach it like it's a problem to "fix". Indeed, it's not up to you to solve anything, even if you think you have answers. Depression is not conquered by logic. It is helped by love. Therefore, don't jump in too quickly with what you think are solutions. The person with depression likely won't hear your advice or ideas until they are ready.

When a person is hurting, how they feel is more important than your "solution" or opinion. It doesn't matter whether you understand how they're feeling or not, either. How they feel is how they feel, so focus on helping with that.

That said, never underestimate the potential of planting a seed. Dealing with depression is a process that takes perseverance over a long time and requires opening up in a supportive environment. So create that environment where the person feels safe to say anything without fear of being judged, confronted, or told what to do. Sometimes people have made a big difference by saying very little and instead just being around to listen patiently. Remember appearances can deceive. A person with depression needs company, needs to talk, and needs support.

> The least helpful thing people have said to me is, "You have depression? But you're always smiling. I would never have guessed." And then they go back to whatever they were doing, as if you hadn't just opened up your soul to them.
>
> — From a valued friend

What the person does not need is insensitive words and acts. Very likely those will trigger a bad response because they go to the heart of what caused the depression.

Talking to someone about their depression can be tricky, for sure. You feel like you're walking on eggshells. Even those of us who carry depression understand how unpredictable our condition can seem. *Seem* is the operative word. There are actually some predictable patterns, at least on the negative side of the ledger. While there are no magic words that can snap someone out of chronic despondency, there are definitely some that can worsen it.

If nothing else, when you talk to a family member, a friend, or a colleague about their depression, remember you are not inside that person's head. You don't live with it. Therefore, listen and learn before you jump in with your take the situation.

> Sometimes it's not what people say so much as how they treat a depressed person. Other times, it's what they say.
>
> — From a valued friend

Crappy un-empathetic things to say

If you say the things listed below to a person with depression – or behind their back – I recommend you learn what depression feels like and make *listening* your default action. For all you know, insensitive words could drive the person closer to self-harm.

- *"But you don't look depressed."*
- *"Get a grip. Snap out of it."*
- *"Just cheer up and be happy."*
- *"You're making me depressed."*
- *"Again?... Still?"*
- *"Nobody helped me when I had problems. Help yourself."*
- *"You're just trying to get attention."*
- *"Can't you just take a pill or something?"*
- *"Who cares?"*
- *"Shut up."*
- *"Go away."*
- *"I'm sick of this."*
- *"I don't want to hear this."*
- *"You're wrong."*
- *"You're useless."*
- *"You need a girlfriend/a boyfriend/a vacation/to get laid."*
- *"It's always 'me, me, me'."*
- *"Depression isn't real."*
- *"You're such a drama queen."*
- *"Are you sure it isn't just PMS?"*
- *"Those pills aren't helping."*
- *"Have a stiff drink or eat some chocolate. That will help."*

And whatever you do, don't take advantage of their state of mind by having sex with them for the first time. Don't even think it's a way to be helpful. (If you're already a couple, sex is a judgment call.)

Words you think will help, but likely won't

Take care with the words listed below. If you know the person very well and have talked about this stuff before, maybe you can say some of these, but still be careful. The general rule is… when in doubt, don't.

- *"I understand."* Do you? Really? That's a big call.
- *"This, too, shall pass."*
- *"Things could be worse… Look on the bright side… You don't have a terminal illness… There are kids starving in the world… There are others much worse off than you… Some real tragedy would put things in perspective."* You'll likely never hear a credible mental health professional say these things. So why would you say them? Maybe you think they work for you, but this problem isn't about you.
- *"What do you have to be depressed about? Things aren't so bad. Your problems aren't that bad."* What matters is how the person feels, not your judgmental perspective.
- Listing your problems, either as a comparison or because you don't want to listen and just want to talk about you.
- *"It's all in your mind."* No shit, Sherlock.
- Shitty platitudes: *"Pick yourself up, dust yourself off… Nobody said life was fair… Stop feeling sorry for yourself…"*
- *"Happiness is a choice."* True, but that doesn't help in the middle of a depressive episode.
- *"Do you go to church? Do you read the Bible?"* Depression already involves so much circular thinking. While your intention may be positive, at this stage the person probably doesn't need more circular thinking that is so common in organized religion.
- *"I'll pray for you."* Maybe a fellow believer will appreciate it, but others may not. It's not about making you feel better.
- *"You can do anything you want. Just apply yourself."* Deep down

the person knows this, but needs to be shown how, often by professionals.

- *"Take a vacation."*
- *"I haven't been well, also."*
- *"I'm annoyed at you that you're always away/late/cancelling appointments."*

Simple things that can make a world of positive difference

Please be supportive, empathetic, and patient. Your slightest act of support could make a huge difference. Remember that a person with depression is usually feeling isolated, needs to talk, and needs support. The person needs friendship, not judgment or investigation. Your goal is to help them open up, not close down.

Here are a few ideas to get you started.

- Invite the person to things: *"Let's go have coffee, or have a meal, or catch a movie."* Don't give up if the answer is no. Try again later.
- *"I love you and believe in you."*
- *"I have a hug for you. Always."*
- Don't ask, *"How are you?"* Ask, *"What are you up to?"* and then be interested and supportive.
- Just catching up and providing support are two of the biggest things that are needed.
- *"You are not alone."*
- *"I'm here. Lean on me."*
- *"I care about you. I value you."*
- *"Do you need someone to listen?"*
- *"I don't know much about depression or what it's about for you, so please tell me."*
- *"There are no wrong emotions. There are just emotions. It's OK for you to have those emotions and feel this way."*
- *"You are strong. I am amazed at your strength."*

- *"Yell at me if you want. I won't give up on you."*
- If you know the person well, something helpful and yet also terrifying to say: *"You need to work on it, and only you can do it."* Follow it up repeatedly with: *"I care about you and value you."*
- *"I can't always be there, but I'll try my best. I'm here now."*
- *"Take your time. I know it doesn't get better overnight. One day at a time. I'll help."*
- *"Talk to a professional. I value you. Do it for me, if not for you. I'll even drive you there and back again."*
- Go for a walk with the person.
- Leave encouraging notes and text messages.

Some friends just kicked me in the ass. But not the rude way. They forced me to go out, see the sun, and meet people. But they always accepted when I canceled.

— From a valued friend

The most AMAZING words I have heard

"I can't begin to understand what you're going through, but I value you enormously. And I feel more alive just by knowing you."

Imagine having a problem and hearing that from another person.

Other simple things that can make a world of difference

- Remember that the person needs friendship, not judgment or investigation.
- Just catching up and providing support are the two biggest things that are needed.
- In-person contact is best. With texts or online communication, your message can be misinterpreted or diluted by everything else the person looks at online. But do whatever you can and don't give up.

When you meet resistance or pushback

When you say some of the positive things above, the depression sufferer might still try to push you away. That's because those of us with depression are conditioned not to believe good things about ourselves. We may even become frustrated and try taking out our hurt on a convenient target – like you. Some of us might rage in response. (I sure have.) Do your best not to take it personally. Remember that the rage is a way of acting out against the people/situation/feelings that are at the root of the depression, not against you. Remain calm, loving, and supportive. The things listed here are helpful, even if the person doesn't show it or if they react the opposite way to what you expect.

A few good tips for how to approach a depressed person

- **The child approach.** As ridiculous or corny as this may seem, apply the same approach as you would with an upset child. I don't mean be condescending. Instead, show love, empathy, compassion, etc. Teach what love is, because the person may have forgotten.
- **Just be there.** Sometimes you don't have to say much, or even anything. Just be there, listen, and support. Offer hugs, coffee, a snack, a walk, some help around the house.
- **Don't abandon.** Keeping away from a suffering person can be devastating, even if they say they want to be alone. Maybe you stay away because you don't know what to say or do. That's understandable. But isolation is a major part of depression. When people lose friendships, relationships and jobs, depression worsens.
- **Listen. Listen. Listen**. Don't jump in with solutions. Help them get it off their chest, at least for now.
- **No ultimatums.** Tough love in the form of an ultimatum does not work. Approaches like "Fix this or get out" or "If this happens again, I'm leaving" are pretty much guaranteed to fail.

Thank you for kindness in helping your loved one climb the mountain.

NINETEEN

Helpful resources

These are just a few resources that I found helpful as I climbed my mountain. If you have any negative reactions or pushback to the ideas of "self-help" books and mentors, like I once did, I ask you to reconsider. After all, this book you're reading is a self-help book.

By all means, find your own materials as well. Not every recommended resource will click for every person.

If you truly want to change and truly want guidance, resources and mentors that are good for you will appear. They did for me.

Kick Ass by Mel Robbins

I recommend listening to all of Mel's audiobooks and podcasts. She is awesome. She's honest and caring and wise, without the bullshit and fluff that you sometimes get with motivational speakers. Listening to her audiobook *Kick Ass* is especially great because you can hear people's profound, visceral reactions as Mel coaches them and helps them confront what's been holding them back. In minutes, she gets these people to go beyond what they thought was their problem and find the true issue. All of them find themselves blown away – in a good way! It's funny, it's inspiring, it's emotional. Above all, you find yourself gaining insight from each person's segment because you can see pieces of yourself in every story.

Mel is direct, insightful, brutally honest, and yet extremely caring. She's one hell of a coach. You'll wish she was interviewing you.

— *Kick Ass with Mel Robbins: Life-Changing Advice from the Author of "The 5 Second Rule"*. Written and narrated by Mel Robbins. An original audiobook published by Audible, 2018.

How to Survive Your Childhood Now That You're an Adult by Ira Israel

This book by psychotherapist Ira Israel is a game changer. It's only 180 pages, so it's not a hard slog. I felt like parts of it had been written specifically for me. Indeed, ever since I serendipitously found it one day and read it, Ira has become a true mentor for me.

This book demonstrates that emotional memories from your early childhood, before you could use words, have a profound effect on how you see yourself in later life. Your attachment with primary caregivers as a pre-verbal infant forms a blueprint for your relationships with others and your relationship with yourself. Ira also examines, from his deep research and experience as a therapist, why our modern way of life is essentially a factory for producing resentment and depression.

Best of all, this book provides some great tools to use for cleansing and rebuilding your life. It's head and shoulders above all other books on mental health and self-help that I have read.

— *How to Survive Your Childhood Now That You're an Adult: A Path to Authenticity and Awakening.* Written by Ira Israel. Published by New World Library, 2017.

Claim Your Power by Mastin Kipp

This book can help you understand yourself more deeply and profoundly than you may have thought possible. It's more than a book, it's a project to get you in touch with your true self. It will guide you how to acknowledge the pain of your past as well as the good things. It takes you through exercises to find the two primary emotions that are your true self and helps you identify your purpose in this life. It's a very encouraging book. You will see clearly what's troubling you – at the core, not just the depression which is a symptom – and also what's awesome in your life. It then provides tools and encouragement to release old wounds and move forward more positively.

I found it in my local library by pure accident. Or perhaps I was guided. The first time I picked it up, I saw that it required 40 days, thought "Ugh!" and put it down. But I came back to it a week later and gave it a try. I knew I had to open my mind to different things, so I went into it with no expectations.

Simply read one chapter per day over 40 days and make notes. I used an exercise book. Some days you make lots of notes, some days hardly any. With Kipp's guidance, you will lay out clearly the problems that are holding you back, the good and bad memories from your life, and your strengths and loves.

You end up with a collection of tremendous reflections and thoughts that you can refer back to many times over.

> — *Claim Your Power: A 40-Day Journey to Dissolve the Hidden Blocks That Keep You Stuck and Finally Thrive in Your Life's Unique Purpose.* Written by Mastin Kipp. Published by Hay House Inc., 2017.

Zero Limits by Joe Vitale and Hew Len

Be advised that saying this book's four key phrases over and over can stir up huge emotions and change. But that's what we depression sufferers need. We have to find a way to work through the difficult emotions and learn how to release the discomfort.

You may think that the words you say in the mantras are just words – and most people think it's stupid and resist doing it – but they have power beyond what you think.

- Forgive me.
- I love you.
- I forgive you.
- Thank you.

It's very much like the Forgive Mantra I describe in the Climb chapter. Psychologists have done so much research into how powerful forgiveness is, to the point that there is even a department at Stanford University dedicated to forgiveness.

If you've had trouble getting through the grief part of depression and forgiving the people around you – and forgiving yourself – this book is another game changer.

— *Zero Limits: The Secret Hawaiian System for Wealth, Health, Peace, and More.* Written by Joe Vitale and Ihaleakala Hew Len. Published by Wiley, 2008.

TED talks

There are so many online and on Netflix. Just follow your heart. I do recommend any and all talks by Brené Brown, an expert on shame and vulnerability. Shame plays a huge role in depression, just as being vulnerable does for overcoming it. Brown is very real and encouraging. I also recommend listening to David Steindl-Rast's beautiful talks about gratitude and happiness.

Just do something

It doesn't matter which resource you start with. It doesn't matter if you think you're ready or not. Just do something to get yourself on a different road. You've been down the old road of depression too many times. You know where it goes and you know that it sucks.

Get reading. Get listening. The sooner new ideas take root, the sooner you can start growing and changing.

Epilogue – Inspiration from my niece

In April 2020, as the world adjusted to quarantine lockdown during the COVID-19 pandemic, my nine-year-old niece Adelaine decided without prompting to write out words of positivity. She had lost her mother to cancer only 14 months earlier. Then, with lockdowns, she was unable to go to school that she loved so much. Yet this beautiful soul would not stop love from being with her and exuding from her. Thank you, Adey.

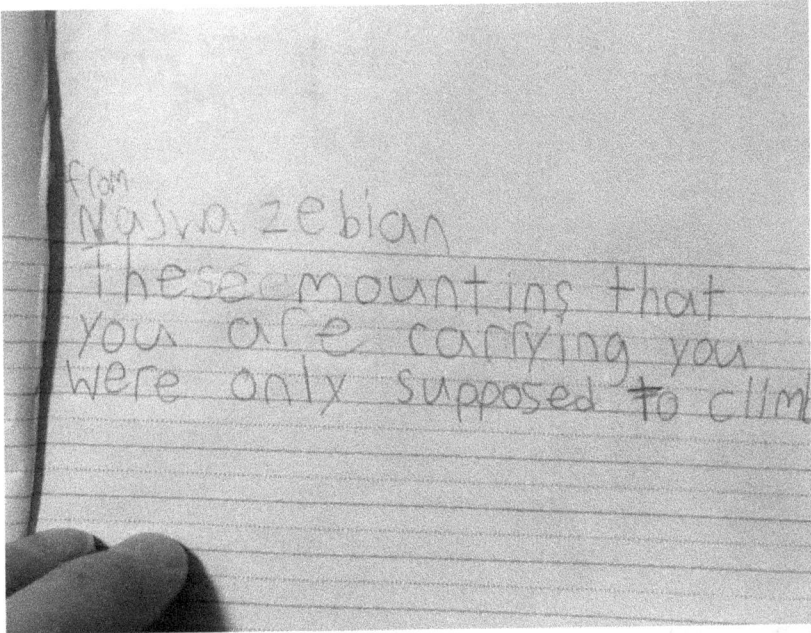

from
Najwa zebian
these mountins that
you are carrying you
were only supposed to clim

from
someone
What consumes your
mind controls your life

From
mr.haagle
Whether you think you can,
or think you can't: you'r
right.

from
someone
Running away from your
problem's is a race you'll
never win.

from
Winston churchill
Attitude is a little
thing that makes a BIG
difference.

from
someone.
Try and fail dont fail
and try.

from
me
You cant be bitter
and expect your life to
be sweet.

from
Book Wonder
You are beutiful no mater
what they say words cant bring
You are beutiful in every
single way no words cant
bring you down

IM POSIBLE

from
John C. Maxwell
Positve thinking must be
followed by positive doing.

from
John Kabat Zinn
you can not stop the
waves but you can learn
how to surf.

from
me
Doors close so better
ones can be open.

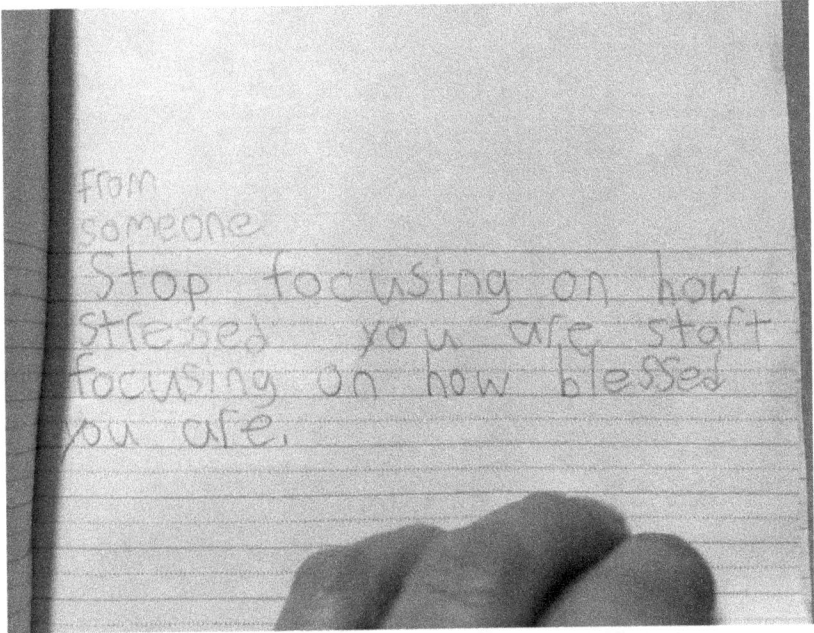

from
someone
Stop focusing on how
stressed you are start
focusing on how blessed
you are.

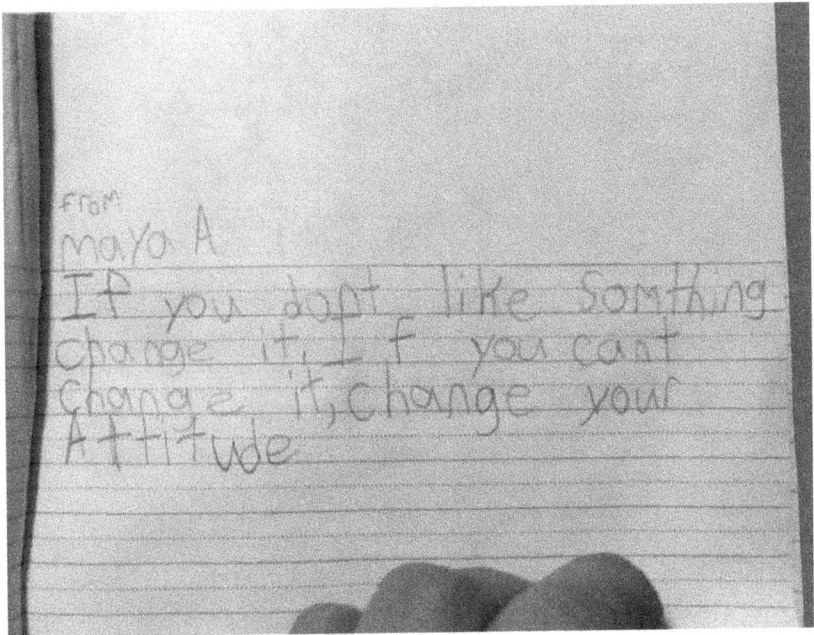

From
maya A
If you dont like somthing
change it, If you cant
change it, change your
Attitude

from
me
It's only a bad day not
a bad life.

dont try to fit, just be
you.

from
someone

Even if you stumble your
still moving forward.

from
Jan Goldstein

turn your face to the
sun and the shadow falls
behinde you.

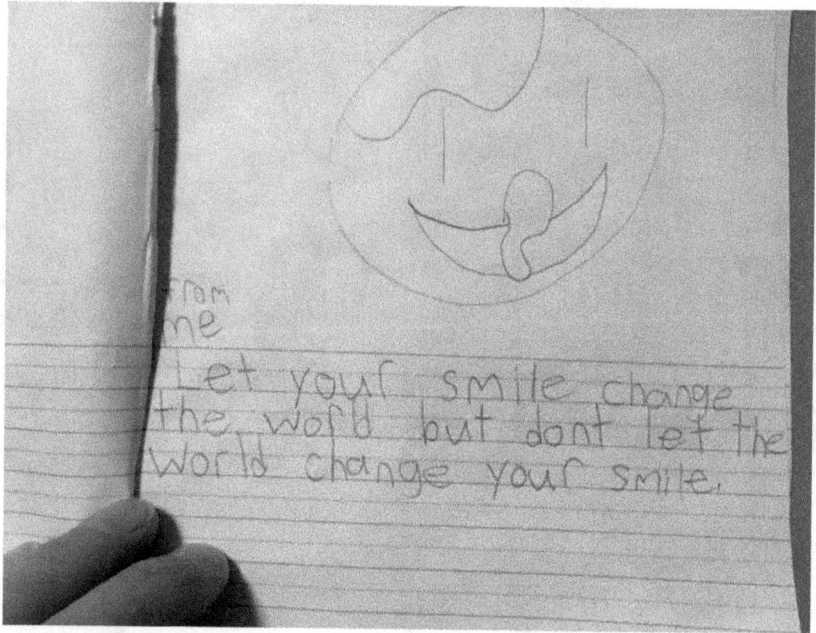

References

Bennie, J. A., Teychenne, M. J., De Cocker, K., & Biddle, S. J. (2019). Associations between aerobic and muscle-strengthening exercise with depressive symptom severity among 17,839 U.S. adults. *Preventive Medicine*, 121-127.

Campbell, J. (1988). Joseph Campbell and the Power of Myth. (B. Moyers, Interviewer)

Centre for Suicide Research, University of Oxford. (2013). *Mindfulness Based Cognitive Therapy and the prevention of relapse in depression*. Retrieved from http://cebmh.warne.ox.ac.uk/csr/mbct.html

Gillihan, S. J. (2019, March 1). *Yes, You Are Lovable With Depression and Anxiety*. Retrieved from WebMD: https://blogs.webmd.com/mental-health/20190301/yes-you-are-lovable-with-depression-and-anxiety

Hari, J. (2018). *Lost Connections: Why You're Depressed and How to Find Hope*. Bloomsbury.

Harris, D., Warren, J., & Adler, C. (2017). *Meditation for Fidgety Skeptics: A 100% Happier How-to Book*. Spiegel & Grau.

Hollis, J. (2001). *Creating a Life: Finding Your Individual Path (Studies in Jungian Psychology by Jungian Analysts)*. Inner City Books.

Hollis, R. (2018). *Girl, Wash Your Face*. Thomas Nelson.

Israel, I. (2017). *How to Survive Your Childhood Now That You're an Adult*. New World Library.

Israel, I. (2018, August 29). *The Magic of Esalen*. Retrieved from iraisrael.com: https://iraisrael.com/the-magic-of-esalen/

Luskin, D. F. (2017, August 16). Forgiveness Is Not What You Think It Is. (L. Seago, Interviewer)

Rilke, R. M. (1929). *Letters to a Young Poet*. W.W. Norton (2004 edition).

Robbins, M. (2018, June 5). *Struggling with depression? 8 strategies you need to know.* Retrieved from melrobbins.com: https://melrobbins.com/struggling-with-depression-8-strategies-you-need-to-know/

Rollins, H. (1998). *The Portable Henry Rollins.* Villard.

Segal, Z. V., Williams, M., & Teasdale, J. (2012). *Mindfulness-Based Cognitive Therapy for Depression (Second Edition).* The Guilford Press.

Staff, M. C. (2017, September 17). *Depression and anxiety: Exercise eases symptoms.* Retrieved from The Mayo Clinic: https://www.mayoclinic.org/diseases-conditions/depression/in-depth/depression-and-exercise/art-20046495#:~:text=Regular%20exercise%20may%20help%20ease,your%20sense%20of%20well%2Dbeing

Strayed, C. (2012). *Wild: From Lost to Found on the Pacific Crest Trail.* Vintage.

Acknowledgments

I am forever grateful to Corinne for her unceasing love and support as I confronted the worst emotional memories associated with my depression. There were many times when she felt scared, overwhelmed, and helpless, yet she never gave up on me. Corinne is an angel who showed me the way back to embracing love.

A huge thank you to Dr. Bali Sohi for being my Sherpa and showing me the pathway up my mountain. Without her remarkable help, I might very well be still stuck in the depths of depression.

This book would not be possible without the help of Ira Israel. After reading his book, I reached out to him on a whim. He has since become a mentor and friend. I have been stunned every step of the way by Ira's extraordinary grace, kindness, generosity, and wisdom.

To every person who has known me and tried to help me through my depression over 39 years, you have my profound thanks. Please forgive me if/when I wronged you in any way.

Most people who have met John Newell know him through his family or from his quartet that won an international a cappella singing championship. In 2018, so many of them were surprised when John announced publicly that he developed depression in 1982 at the age of 12 and had carried it ever since. As is very common with depression sufferers, John had become adept at hiding the condition and living with it in mental and emotional isolation.

In 2016, after 34 years of being unable to break depression's hold over him, John went to a psychologist to tackle it head on. Despite not knowing what he was getting into or where he was headed, he worked hard over the next five years to do what his psychologist asked. John now lives a happier life because he understands his depression better and keeps working at improving his mental wellness each day.

John was born and raised in Australia before moving to Canada where he lives with his wife and three children. He is the author of *Let It Out*, a book describing his singing approach and philosophy.

Be patient toward all that is unsolved in your heart and try to love the questions themselves, like locked rooms and like books that are now written in a very foreign tongue. Do not now seek the answers, which cannot be given you because you would not be able to live them. And the point is, to live everything. *Live* the questions now. Perhaps you will then gradually, without noticing it, live along some distant day into the answer.

— Rainer Maria Rilke